Additional Praise for

THE ENTREPRENEURIAL SCHOLAR

"At first blush, the realms of scholarship and entrepreneurship may seem in tension, even oxymoronic. In this illuminating book, Ilana Horwitz details the many links between these practices and, in the process, illuminates both."

—HOWARD GARDNER, author of *Frames of Mind* and coauthor of *The Real World of College*

"Ilana Horwitz shows how an entrepreneurial mindset can help scholars enhance their reach and impact. She offers an inspiring vision for the roles of scholars and scholarship in today's world."

—DANIEL R. PORTERFIELD, author of *Mindset Matters: The Power of College to Activate Lifelong Growth*

"Every graduate student is the CEO of their own education. In this vital, bracing book, Ilana Horwitz shows how to do that job. *The Entrepreneurial Scholar* is filled with good stories—including Horwitz's own—that point to how entrepreneurial thinking can unlock creativity you didn't know you had. If you're in graduate school or thinking of going, or if you teach graduate students, you should read this book."

—LEONARD CASSUTO, coauthor of *The New PhD: How to Build a Better Graduate Education*

"Ilana Horwitz has provided a valuable service to the profession. This book empowers graduate students to apply their skills to solving real-world problems. With her approach, they will see themselves as active agents in their education and careers."

—ZACHARY SHORE, author of *Grad School Essentials*

THE ENTREPRENEURIAL
SCHOLAR

SKILLS FOR SCHOLARS

A list of titles in the series appears at the back of the book.

The Entrepreneurial Scholar

Scholar

A NEW MINDSET FOR SUCCESS
IN ACADEMIA AND BEYOND

ILANA M. HORWITZ

PRINCETON UNIVERSITY PRESS

PRINCETON & OXFORD

Copyright © 2025 by Princeton University Press

Princeton University Press is committed to the protection of copyright and the intellectual property our authors entrust to us. Copyright promotes the progress and integrity of knowledge. Thank you for supporting free speech and the global exchange of ideas by purchasing an authorized edition of this book. If you wish to reproduce or distribute any part of it in any form, please obtain permission.

Requests for permission to reproduce material from this work should be sent to permissions@press.princeton.edu

Published by Princeton University Press
41 William Street, Princeton, New Jersey 08540
99 Banbury Road, Oxford OX2 6JX

press.princeton.edu

All Rights Reserved

ISBN 9780691240886
ISBN (pbk.) 9780691240893
ISBN (e-book) 9780691240909

British Library Cataloging-in-Publication Data is available

Editorial: Matt Rohal and Alena Chekanov
Production Editorial: Nathan Carr
Jacket/Cover Design: Chris Ferrante
Production: Lauren Reese
Publicity: Tyler Hubbert and Kathryn Stevens
Copyeditor: Anne Sanow

Jacket/Cover Credit: Cover illustration by Marcella Macalalag

This book has been composed in Arno

10 9 8 7 6 5 4 3 2 1

To my parents, Cecilia and Michael (z"l) Straznik,
who taught me the value of perseverance
and the power of entrepreneurial thinking.

CONTENTS

THE ENTREPRENEURIAL
SCHOLAR

Introduction

THIS BOOK IS intended to help you think like an entrepreneurial scholar. By entrepreneurial, I'm talking about the skill of crafting something fresh—like knowledge—out of scant resources amid the fog of uncertainty. Thinking like an entrepreneur means asking yourself: *Given who I am, what I know, and who I know, what kind of opportunities could I create for myself?*[1]

This isn't your typical guide on the mechanics of earning a doctorate or navigating the academic job market.[2] Instead, *The Entrepreneurial Scholar* invites you to see scholarship through a new lens. It's a manual for those at the dawn of their scholarly journey, be they doctoral candidates or postdocs, to embrace an entrepreneurial approach in both academia and beyond. It's also a fresh perspective for early to mid-career faculty seeking innovative paths in their professional journey. This book isn't about the "how-tos" of academia; it's about reimagining what it means to be a scholar—a new mindset for academic success.

———————

This book grew out of an idea I wrote about during graduate school. In my last semester, I audited a class called "Writing for a Public Audience." It was taught by Sam Wineburg, a professor I greatly admired for his scholarship on historical thinking and digital literacy, but also for his highly accessible and engaging writing style. Like him, I wanted to produce knowledge that reached beyond academic journals, so I was eager to learn about the world of public scholarship.

Unsurprisingly, the primary assignment for the class was to write an op-ed. Most students wrote about their research, but I felt a burning desire to write about my PhD journey. In the months approaching graduation, I constantly thought about how my experience had changed me and tried to make sense of my circuitous route to academia. I felt simultaneously demoralized that I did not have an academic job lined up (despite two attempts on the job market), but also incredibly proud of myself for completing my six-year journey. My friends and family can attest that it was a peculiar and surprising career move, which up to that point had included stints in start-ups, management consulting, teaching, and research/evaluation firms. To tell the truth, academic pursuits had never been my thing: I had not been an exceptionally good high school or college student, and a series of failures in the workplace made me seriously question my intellectual abilities. But in the months leading up to my graduation, I kept returning to the same question: Why did it seem like I enjoyed the PhD journey more than many of my peers?

My journey to publishing that op-ed was not smooth. When I first penned the piece in 2019 it faced several rejections, and for the next two years, it lay dormant on my computer while I focused on other pursuits.

In June 2021, with only a few weeks before starting my position at Tulane, I looked at my remaining to-do list. Prominently featured at the top and not yet crossed off was the op-ed. I cringed as I reread the article, thinking about its history of rejection. I knew the piece needed a reframe, so I asked myself: Who am I? What do I know? My nontraditional path to academia gave me the expertise to make an unusual case to graduate students: think more like entrepreneurs.

———

Now I just needed to find someone to publish it. Thinking about that meant asking another entrepreneurial question: Who do I know? I had already published one op-ed in *Inside Higher Ed*, and since I had a relationship with an editor, I decided to start there. Much to my surprise, the new piece was accepted within hours of submission.

The argument I put forth in my op-ed was that shifting from a consumer to a producer of knowledge fundamentally changed my relationship with education. To be clear, I did not start graduate school thinking of myself as a knowledge producer, but my background and experiences certainly primed me for this shift. Like most graduate students, I expected to consume a lot of information while suffering through several years of reading to write something mysterious called a dissertation. But at my graduate school orientation, Dr. Eamonn Callan, a philosopher of education, gave my incoming class advice that changed my paradigm for learning: "Your job is no longer to consume knowledge. Your job is to produce it."

This shift from consumer to producer allowed me to think of myself as an entrepreneur of ideas. In invoking the language of entrepreneurialism, I am referring to *the ability to generate something new (in this case, knowledge) with limited resources in a highly uncertain environment*. And after six years of training myself to be a knowledge producer, my op-ed argued that this kind of approach to academia was not just valuable—it was essential for both surviving and even flourishing. The op-ed was accepted at *Inside Higher Ed* and published with the title "Why PhD Students Should Think Like Entrepreneurs."[3]

Throughout the next week, I received several emails from professors (several of whom worked as graduate student directors) and even a therapist who worked with grad students telling me that this was a much-needed perspective their students would benefit from and how excited they were to share it. Like any academic, I love hearing from readers who appreciate my ideas, and knowing that what I wrote was helpful was particularly gratifying.

Then I opened a most unexpected email: it was from Peter Dougherty, an editor at Princeton University Press, asking if I'd be interested in fleshing out the op-ed into a book. Writing it would require gathering quite a lot of data from figures in and out of academia spanning multiple disciplines and industries from a wide range of sources—many of whom I didn't know. It would mean moving beyond graduate students to speak to the concerns of women scholars alongside first generation/low-income (FLI) and Black, Indigenous, and People of Color (BIPOC) scholars and even consider the needs of mid-career scholars. I quickly realized that writing such a book would ironically require an entrepreneurial approach because I would have to leverage who I was, what I knew, and who I knew. But I was game, because at the end of the day I deeply believe that articulating such an approach is needed.

Why Academics Today Need an Entrepreneurial Approach

Some aspects of entrepreneurialism are quite familiar to academics, like operating with finite resources in contexts where success is anything but certain. Academia is unpredictable because the nature of academic employment has become profoundly precarious over the past few decades. Certainly, for graduate students, the traditional apprenticeship model of doctoral education is not working the way it used to,[4] and it is unlikely that an advanced degree will automatically lead to a secure and prestigious academic career.[5] Most people who pursue PhDs have a slim chance of becoming professors, especially professors on the tenure track.[6] Only one in twenty will get a tenure-track job. It has also become very unclear what it takes to get such a job. When I was a graduate student, in sociology of education from 2013 to 2019, a job-market candidate with a solo-authored publication in a top journal would have very good job prospects in my field. But today a candidate with this profile might not even make a shortlist, much less be offered a position.

The pervasive sense of doom regarding one's prospects is abundantly clear in the dozens of essays that make up the

"Quit Lit" genre—farewells to academia from grad students through tenured professors.[7] Take for example Rebecca Schuman's (PhD, literature) well-known 2013 "thesis hatement" published in *Slate*:

> During graduate school, you will be broken down and re-configured in the image of the academy. By the time you finish—if you even do—your academic self will be the culmination of your *entire* self, and thus you will believe, incomprehensibly, that not having a tenure-track job makes you worthless. You will believe this so strongly that when you do not land a job, it will destroy you, and nobody outside of academia will understand why. (Bright side: You will no longer have any friends outside academia.)[8]

The problem is that PhD programs rarely provide their students with a sense of the diverse kinds of career opportunities available to graduates.[9] This means that while most PhDs will not end up in academia, they also do not know what else to do with themselves.

It doesn't help that for many doctoral students their professional persona is tied to their sense of self, and not getting an academic job is proof that they are simply not deserving of success. This perspective is well-articulated by Melissa Dalgleish (PhD, Canadian literature) in her 2013 "I Quit" Letter:[10]

> If I finished my PhD and didn't become a professor, as I was pretty certain I would not become, I would be nothing. My identity was so tied up with being an academic that contemplating not being one was something like contemplating my own death . . . My desperate desire to stay in

academe turned into fury at the system that had taught me that my self-worth lay in conforming to its standards, that those PhDs who didn't become academics were second-class citizens, lesser, unworthy.

If most graduate programs do little to inform students of jobs outside of academia, it's no surprise they do even less to prepare graduates for such nonacademic jobs. When I spoke with Teresa Mangum, who is a professor in the Departments of Gender, Women's, and Sexuality Studies and English at the University of Iowa and has held several administrative roles both on her campus and with national organizations, she confirmed that most graduate programs only imagine that what they have to offer is training for the professoriate. When they advertise their departments, they talk about where people got placed in academia and indicate who ended up in other jobs. At the same time, she notes that it's never occurred to PhDs that what they are doing could prepare them for a myriad of career paths. This is why Mangum is currently directing an initiative funded by the Mellon Foundation called Humanities for the Public Good (HPG), which supports faculty in transforming courses and curricula in existing humanities PhD programs to support the values of HPG and offers a certificate program for students who want to focus on preparing for diverse careers.

Graduate education certainly needs to change, but my goal here is not to propose changes to the system of doctoral education and academia more broadly. Others like Leonard Cassuto have done this quite well. As he has persuasively argued, graduate programs need to "revamp their curricula, structures, and standards in a way that prepares today's graduate students for a wider range of employment."[11] He is not alone. As Leanne Horinko, James Van Wyck, and Jordan Reed observe in their book *The Reimagined PhD*, "Doctoral education is a tool in the hand of the user, not the creation of a tool to be used in a system. PhDs are not created for a specific purpose, namely the tenure track. PhDs must be equipped for a variety of purposes, which they must have wide leeway to construct for themselves."[12]

This advice resonates with people like Tamara Gilkes Borr, a colleague who was completing her PhD at the same time as I was. Frustrated by many elements of academia, Borr ultimately decided to pursue a job at Boston Consulting Group and then became the public policy correspondent for *The Economist*. As she remarked when speaking about her experience,

> We need to think of careers outside academia not so much as the failed path but as another great option for a system that is going to create "extra" people. I wish I had allowed myself the freedom to decide that a job outside academia wasn't a "last resort." It took me a ridiculously sad amount of time to realize how awesome the alternatives to academia are. I wish I'd known that [taking such a job] wasn't failure.

But waiting for academia to undergo slow, self-initiated reform is not what entrepreneurs do. So instead of just adding my voice to those who are already working from the inside to change things, I want to empower scholars with an entrepreneurial approach given the system that we *have*—not bemoan the absence of the system we *wish* we had.

What Entrepreneurialism Is and Is Not

Entrepreneurship is a way of thinking, acting, and being that combines the ability to find or create new opportunities with the courage to act on them in a highly uncertain environment.

Some readers might balk at the notion of taking an entrepreneurial approach to scholarship. After all, an entrepreneur is often a term used to describe a for-profit business owner, some of whom have been unethical in their business practices. While Uber and Theranos serve as recent cautionary tales about the perils of start-up culture and vivid examples of how blind worship of start-up founders can go wildly wrong,[13] there is a sense of purity among some academics who believe they are above anything monetary—that pursuing intellectual endeavors is a selfless endeavor and people who run for-profit businesses are necessarily selfish.

But entrepreneurs are rarely concerned about making millions when they first come up with their ideas. They are more focused on solving some problem, and many have changed the world in amazing ways, largely thanks to insights developed by . . . yes, academics. Consider the field of computer science. The internet, Amazon, GPS, smartphones—it's hard to name a modern information technology innovation and not directly tie it back to academic work that was done in the last twenty to thirty years in universities. When I say that scholars should think like entrepreneurs, I do not mean that they should try to generate a profit or monetize their work. What I am proposing is that their insights should be used for good—to inform policies, practices, and even products where applicable. My advocacy for an entrepreneurial mindset is not about glorifying entrepreneurs, but rather about prompting scholars to adopt a new mindset. Thinking like an entrepreneur can help scholars consider the broader impact of their research and how it can contribute to society.

Nor is it my intention in discussing entrepreneurship to advocate for a neoliberal approach that advocates for the corporatization of academia. In my view, the current prevalence of corporate language within the university—which includes terms like technology transfer, knowledge economy, grant generation, and the all-purpose focus on efficiency—wrongly dominates academic scholarship both within and outside institutions. As Maggie Berg and Barbara Seeber so ably discuss in *The Slow Professor*, this focus on productivity and accountability has negative consequences for both the quality of scholarship and the working lives of academics.[14] They observe that privileging certain forms of knowledge and emphasizing metrics naturally leads to a faster pace of research that devalues deep understanding and reflection. Furthermore, the pressure to be productive and marketable undermines the collegial culture of academia and contradicts the core values of intellectual advancement and discovery. Berg and Seeber advocate for a slower, more reflective approach to research that values nurturing and revising our grasp of a topic rather than simply accumulating new information.

In arguing that scholars should adopt an entrepreneurial approach, I am also not arguing in support of the idea of applying market models to universities (known as "academic capitalism") or the intensification of pressure to attract external funding and produce knowledge that is immediately applicable to the needs of the private and/or government sectors (known as "research capitalism").[15] Nor do I endorse the idea of scholars operating like business-oriented research firms, where research tasks are restricted to specific periods and are conducted through fee-for-service models. The academic research model provides scholars the time needed to consider multiple perspectives and delve into their data. Augusta Rohrbach articulated this idea clearly in *The Reimagined PhD* when she observed that academics are not constrained by the business calendar and can pursue knowledge for its own sake.[16] This approach encourages innovative thinking and the pursuit of truth, which is a valuable contribution to society.

Maybe it's reassuring to discover that the field of business sees optimizing processes and avoiding failure as *managerial* issues. Focusing on that kind of thinking works best in times of certainty when goals are predetermined, issues are transparent, and information is reliable and accessible. Entrepreneurship is in many respects the opposite of management. Entrepreneurs face considerably more uncertainty and have a lot less information than managers. They are forced to use the resources they have rather than wait for more to show up while navigating unchartered waters.[17] Entrepreneurial thinking is about experimentation combined with embracing and leveraging failure. If management is about learning to act, then entrepreneurship is about acting to learn.

Curiously enough, the incentive structure for US faculty encourages individual professors to be entrepreneurial in their approach, because historically colleges have been fairly autonomous institutions.[18] US higher education emerged in the nineteenth century under unique conditions—when the market was strong, the state was weak, and the church was divided.[19] Colleges were private not-for-profit enterprises that had a state charter but little or no state funding—autonomous enterprises that had found a way to survive without steady support from either church or state. They had to attract and retain students in order to bring in tuition dollars, and they had to make themselves useful both to these students and to elites in the local community, both of whom would then make donations to continue the colleges in operation.[20]

Although this autonomy was a historical accident and not part of a master plan, by the twentieth century it became a major source of strength. More responsive to consumers and community than to the state, institutions managed to mitigate the kind of top-down governance that might have stifled the system's creativity. As a result, the incentive structure for US faculty encourages individual professors to be entrepreneurial. It's true that they need to publish in order to win honors for themselves (and their school). But at its best, the university is a place that gives maximum freedom for faculty to pursue their interests and passions in the justified hope that they will frequently come up with something interesting and possibly even useful, even if its value is not immediately apparent.[21]

This is why I think there's room within the academy for scholars to still take charge of their career path. They cannot predict the future, but they can help create it. They cannot control whether they will land a tenure-track job or get a promotion, but they have agency in what they create with their research. Adopting an entrepreneurial approach will help them embrace and confront uncertainty and reclaim their autonomy.

Growing Up with an Entrepreneurial Approach

Although the realization that academia is well-suited to individuals with an entrepreneurial mindset only occurred to me once I was in graduate school, I had been surrounded by and even forced to embrace such an approach at an early age. I grew up in the former Soviet Union during the 1980s. Under communism, Jews like my family were persecuted, prevented from getting certain jobs, and faced jail time if they were caught practicing their faith. Ironically, the former Soviet Union didn't want the Jews to emigrate because they had high levels of education. My parents tried for almost a decade to find a way out, and in 1988 we finally received permission to emigrate as refugees. When I was seven years old, we packed up four suitcases (the maximum we were allowed to take) and left.

Finding our way in the US with no English skills and very limited financial resources meant that my parents were always thinking entrepreneurially: *Given who we are, what we know, and who we know, what kind of opportunities could we create for ourselves?*[22] A relative gave us an old two-door red hatchback car and we moved in with my aunt while we investigated permanent housing options. Eventually, we found a small apartment in Northeast Philadelphia, which we furnished with items that other people had left by the curb or dumpster.

My parents also had to use the means available to them to make ends meet. Like many immigrants, they could not continue to work in their former occupations as engineers in the US. My father found an assembly job at an electrical manufacturing company and my mother started doing janitorial work. Money was tight, so my father would join my mother and put in a second shift after his day job was done. In the evenings, I accompanied my parents to their cleaning jobs in office buildings, where I would dust offices and help empty garbage cans before falling asleep on the lobby couch.

My parents continued to think entrepreneurially. They were extremely handy, so after a few years of scrimping and saving they came up with the idea of buying a cheap fixer-upper house, renovating it, and then renting it. They managed to purchase a house and did all the renovations themselves—which meant that I now spent my evenings and weekends accompanying them to Home Depot. After they renovated one house and rented it, they bought a second one, and then a third. But just as my family was starting to experience some modicum of stability, my father was killed in a car accident. I was a few months shy of my fifteenth birthday and my mother was on her own. I didn't have a choice—now it was time for me to start acting entrepreneurially.

After my father died, I found ways to leverage who I was, what I knew, and who I knew to create opportunities to earn money. There was a Jewish Community Center (JCC) within walking distance of our house, so in ninth grade I got a job working at the front desk. After tenth grade, I leveraged my social networks to find a summer job as a nanny in NYC, and after eleventh grade, another friend's dad helped me get a summer job doing administrative work for a law firm. In twelfth grade, I got a weekend job distributing samples at Philadelphia festivals (my favorite was passing out Pepcid AC to hungover revelers at the 1999 Mummers Day parade).

Having lived a life of uncertainty, I saw college as a means to an end—a way to climb the socioeconomic ladder. My mother made it clear that we were not taking out loans for me to "find myself" or take classes in whatever I found interesting—that was something my affluent peers could afford to do. I didn't think I had the skills or stomach for law or medical school, so I majored in business administration and continued to think creatively about how to make money on the side. I worked as a Hebrew school teacher, tutor, baby-sitter, program planner for the study abroad office, and a photographer for fraternity and sorority events and for corporate parties around Atlanta.

After graduation I experimented with several types of jobs and experiences, always thinking like an entrepreneur about how I could be exposed to new ideas and encounters despite limited resources. I worked at two tech start-ups, and eventually moved to DC to work in international development, where I helped deploy hundreds of subject matter experts to Afghanistan and Iraq to rebuild their education, financial, and political systems.

After a few years of consulting, I started thinking about other career options. I wanted to find a way to combine my passion for education, my enthusiasm for Excel spreadsheets, and my interest in international development. In DC, a master's was necessary for any professional advancement, so I considered returning to school for a degree in international education. But I didn't have a great college GPA and certainly didn't have any college professors whom I could ask for a recommendation. So I came up with a plan: I would enroll in one evening class at the George Washington University and hopefully develop a relationship with a professor who would write me a recommendation. Taking a class would also help me see if I was interested in graduate school in the first place. My plan worked—the professor wrote me a letter of recommendation and I leveraged that to get into a master's program at Teachers College, Columbia University.

I didn't have any plan to continue to a PhD, so I spent the following five years working for a series of research and evaluation firms in DC and the Bay Area. What propelled me back into academia was a series of professional struggles in my late twenties. I didn't feel motivated to work for others on a 9 to 5 schedule but wanted to work for myself so that I had more control over my life. I assumed I would start my own business and I believed that having a PhD would lend credibility to my ventures. So back to school I went. Oh, and did I mention that I started graduate school with an eight-month-old baby?

Seeing Scholarship as an Entrepreneurial Activity

It was during my second year at Stanford that I began to realize how much I enjoyed graduate school. It was completely not what I expected, but everything that I needed. I *was* finally my own boss—something that for many years I had been yearning for. Although my advisor and committee members had control over whether I passed the different requirements, no one told me what to do, when to do it, or how to do it. I noticed that many of my peers found this debilitating, but I found it liberating. Like them, my educational experience up to that point had involved being evaluated on my ability to consume and regurgitate information. But as a doctoral student, I was being asked to produce new information—and that was exhilarating. Producing knowledge meant that everything I read and wrote about had a *purpose* beyond a grade.

What I realized is that thriving in a PhD program isn't about being a good student in the traditional sense. *It is about finding and crafting something original with limited resources, such as time, funding, or materials, while facing an unclear and unpredictable future.* This is what I had been learning and practicing most of my life. It is also the definition of entrepreneurship.

What surprised me is that most doctoral students don't think of themselves as entrepreneurs—they think of themselves as good students. And they are. But they wrongly assume that the same formula that got them through school and college will work in graduate school and later in academia. The first few semesters of grad school are generally smooth sailing as students spend most of their time taking required classes. The routine feels familiar—reminiscent of the script they adhered to for decades. But eventually, that script comes to an end. There are no required classes to attend. No weekly papers to write. No exams to take. As the structure of schooling disappears, students start to feel lost and confused.[23] Emily Roberts, who earned her PhD in bioengineering, described her struggle to understand what the academic enterprise was all about:

> I didn't really understand what we're all here to do and what the goals are beyond just passing your classes and doing some experiments. I see now that it all has to come together to be a picture and a story that you push out, but I don't

think I understood that soon enough, or well enough . . . If I really understood what the point of all of this was, there could have been less burnout in the middle years of graduate school. The burnout came from feeling like I was spinning my wheels, like I wasn't really making progress in the right direction.

What happened to these previous stellar students? What plagues them is the mistaken belief that being a good scholar means being a good *consumer* of information—someone who is a close reader and able to process large volumes of information. But this isn't the right mindset for becoming a scholar. Dr. Callan was right: a graduate student's job is to *produce* knowledge.

Producing knowledge requires an entirely different kind of skillset than consuming information. It's the skillset of an entrepreneur. For example, being entrepreneurial encourages you to take more charge of your life and create opportunities for yourself despite an unknown future. To navigate the uncertainty of academia, it helps to think like an entrepreneur, asking: *How can I use my intellectual capital (knowledge, expertise, and ideas), human capital (skills, talents, and experiences), and social capital (networks, relationships, and connections) to create something*? In other words, how can I combine my knowledge, skills, and networks to create something valuable?

Saras Sarasvathy, a scholar of entrepreneurship at the University of Virginia's Darden School of Business, calls this "effectual thinking."[24] Effectual thinking is means-driven—it starts with what one has (resources, abilities, and aspirations) and focuses on selecting among possible outcomes that can be created with those means. Effectual thinking is adaptive in nature—it assumes that the future is unpredictable and that success comes from being able to leverage contingencies and new opportunities as they arise. Sarasvathy contrasts this with "causal thinking," which is goal oriented—it starts with a pre-determined goal and focuses on identifying the optimal means to achieve that goal. Causal thinking is predictive in nature—it assumes that the future is predictable, and that careful planning can control outcomes. Entrepreneurs often succeed not by predicting the future, but by making use of what they have at hand and working (often with others) to shape the future.

To use a cooking analogy, causal thinking is akin to following a recipe: one starts with a clear picture of the desired outcome—say an authentic Louisiana gumbo—and then gathers the specific ingredients and follows precise steps to achieve it. Effectual thinking, however, is more like improvisational cooking: one begins with the ingredients on hand, and without a fixed outcome in mind, creatively combines them into a dish. You might end up with a gumbo, or a stew, or some other flavorful concoction. Graduate students should see themselves like a chef who starts with the ingredients they have, and begins to create based on what's at hand, realizing that they can diverge from the recipe to create something amazing and new. Entrepreneurs use effectual thinking to start new ventures by imagining possibilities that originate from their means but aren't set on one goal (gumbo) but rather the desired outcome (dinner).

Effectual thinkers also invite the surprise factor because they realize that things happen. Instead of spending time thinking about all the possible "what-if" scenarios to deal with worst-case scenarios, they interpret "bad" news and surprises as potential clues to pivot to a more rewarding outcome. When predicting the future, effectual thinkers start by focusing on what they can control. If their actions don't yield the desired outcomes, they remain resourceful, flexible, and adapt—much like the classic "breakfast for dinner" scenario. An effectual entrepreneur realizes that because we can adapt to the future, we don't need to predict it. This is because they believe that the future is not set, and therefore is created rather than predicted.

Most scholars don't realize they already are flirting with an entrepreneurial mindset. While they're not out to make a profit, scholars spend years ideating, honing, marketing, and disseminating their product: ideas. Generating these ideas often happens with limited resources while navigating a highly uncertain environment. As Scott Cowen, former president of Tulane University, told me, "I don't care if you're a sociologist, or if you're in finance, your role is not just to churn out papers and research. Being a professor is thinking about being entrepreneurial—[to] come up with new ideas that will make the world a better place." Lots of academics have good ideas, but getting those ideas out into the world requires a mindset that is more common among entrepreneurs than among people who are good at school.

Consider the case of John List,[25] who was pursuing a PhD in economics at the University of Wyoming. During graduate school, List attended baseball card conventions to work as a dealer, and he started experimenting with different ways to make money. He would try to negotiate in different ways, bargain in different ways, sell goods in different ways, and buy, sell, and trade differently at different moments in the convention. His deep knowledge and experience of the baseball card market also made him question some of the ideas he was learning in his classes about how economists were making inferences based on lab experiments. List thought there was more value in conducting field experiments, and started to think about how his experiences could be leveraged in his research.

There was just one problem—his professors were not on board. They had very specific ideas and models of what economics research should look like, and field experiments were not in the mix. That forced List to think creatively about how to conduct field experiments without financial resources or the backing of his advisors. He wanted to understand how background characteristics such as age, gender, and race influenced markets, and realized that the very experience that triggered his ideas in the first place—baseball card conventions—gave him the perfect opportunity to randomize people into treatment and control groups. At these conventions, close to a thousand different sellers stand behind six-foot seller tables, selling, trading, and buying cards from customers. List would recruit customers as they walked through the front door and take them to a separate room he had reserved. If customers agreed to participate in the experiment, he would send them to negotiate with various dealers throughout the marketplace. Afterward, they would return to report on what they bought or sold and describe how the negotiations unfolded with different dealers. Unlike in lab experiments, where people know their choices are being scrutinized and can modify their own behavior in socially desirable ways, the sellers at the conventions had no idea they were "in" an experiment. This made it possible for List to examine whether the same seller would, for example, treat a male customer differently than a female customer. Beginning with this early research on a shoestring budget, List launched a revolution in field experiments and helped fuel their explosion over the last twenty-five years.

Entrepreneurialism and the Life of the Mind

My goal in this book is to encourage scholars to become more entrepreneurial in their scholarly endeavors—regardless of where they end up occupationally. Throughout this book, I do not define success as getting an academic job. Very few people will end up in these roles. I argue that scholars who bring an entrepreneurial mindset will feel motivated to write and contribute their ideas to society regardless of where they ultimately land.

Some people begin their graduate studies with the intention to move into nonacademic jobs (I certainly did), while others pursue nonacademic jobs when they realize that academia will not work for them. But academia is not the only place that offers a career rooted in the "life of the mind."[26] As the editors of *The Reimagined PhD* argue, society needs the insights of PhDs, and in turn, PhD programs must adopt a more global perspective. The skills of interpretation, research, discovery, and knowledge are essential across all sectors. We need to reimagine the PhD so that we can broaden the impact of academic learning across society. Any examination of social issues that overlooks the contributions of history, the arts, religion, philosophy, anthropology, and similar fields, as well as the natural sciences, is likely to be superficial and prone to flawed conclusions. In STEM, the concept of technology transfer involves applying academic discoveries to real-world applications. This principle should be extended to the humanities, arts, and social sciences. In their words, "While we might worry that thinking more about applicability sacrifices the traditional intellectual virtue of standing apart from the mainstream society in order to critique it, why should we settle for *critiquing* when we might play a far greater role in *constructing* the public world?"[27]

Instead of a how-to guide to help scholars land an academic job or finish their dissertation, this book spells out an approach that can help them change their perception of what getting and having a PhD entails. It argues that success goes beyond mastering a subject area; it's about using your expertise to generate influential ideas amidst resource limitations and uncertainty.

Developing the habits to be productive and motivated entrepreneurial scholars requires academics to fundamentally rethink their relationship with academia. It's no mystery that academia is rife with uncertainty: expectations are unclear, many advisors are inattentive, no one knows what the academic job market will look like when they graduate, and rarely do scholars feel like they have adequate resources. But these conditions also offer an opportunity to think strategically about the resources and skills available to create a new idea—to be an entrepreneur.

Life outside academia adds another layer of uncertainty during this period, as individuals navigate the complexities of dating, marriage, and childrearing. I had planned to have a second baby between my second and third year of graduate school, strategically timing the arrival to avoid the tumult of a very difficult sequence of econometrics classes. However, life, with its inherent unpredictability, had other plans. It took me a year to get pregnant, and as a result, I had my baby just as that demanding sequence of classes was set to begin. This unexpected turn of events was a stark reminder that we can plan and strategize, but ultimately, we must be prepared to adapt and find creative solutions amidst the fog of uncertainty that life presents.

I see this entrepreneurial approach as offering an added benefit for many scholars who are oftentimes marginalized within the academy.[28] I am advocating for this mindset and writing this book to get a variety of scholars—graduate students, early career scholars, women, FLI and BIPOC scholars, and even mid-career scholars who feel stalled—to see themselves as active agents in their education and careers. Too often, these individuals feel disempowered.[29] The existing structures in the academy, including the power dynamics between advisors and advisees, admittedly limit the ability of doctoral students to apply some of what I am suggesting. But while an individual scholar cannot easily change the structure of the academic profession, they can shift their approach to take agency in areas where they do have control.

For example, I hope this approach is useful for those who are first-generation students or who grew up with limited resources. It's well-known that many people who enter academia also come from economic privilege[30] and have lived lives marked by a sense of stability, security, and confidence. A recent study found that 50 percent of people who earned a

PhD between 2010 and 2018 had at least one parent with a graduate degree.[31] At the other end of the spectrum, only 26 percent of PhD recipients across fields were first-generation college graduates. They have fewer resources at their disposal and might not have parents who can help support them financially during graduate school, unlike their wealthier classmates.[32]

FLI scholars also likely do not know the "rules of the game" when it comes to graduate school. When people grow up with academic family members, they are more familiar with the hidden curriculum of graduate school and have been socialized into the academic world at a young age.[33] Shantel Martinez, a first-generation woman of color, recalls being in her graduate program in communication and media studies at the University of Illinois Urbana-Champaign with peers who were children of professors. "They were reading Foucault at age eighteen, and I was like—what? How is that even possible?"[34] But taking an entrepreneurial mindset turns not knowing the graduate school script into an asset. When I spoke with Constantina Katsari, a tech entrepreneur who received her PhD in history, she put it like this:

> If you come from a working-class background like I did, you don't have any information at all, and you have to get the information from scratch . . . there's a whole load of things that you have no clue about. You need to figure it out for yourself, and this is what entrepreneurs do. Entrepreneurs do not read books and then go out there and implement what they learn from the books. They have to understand the conditions on the ground, they have to understand how

people are thinking, and then they have to understand what needs to be done.

In other words, if you aren't wedded to the norms and expectations, you have a greater sense that you can chart your own path. If you grew up with or have experienced economic insecurity, you already know how to navigate risk and uncertainty and work with limited resources. Most importantly, you already understand how to start small with what you have rather than waiting for what you need. This is all part of entrepreneurial thinking, and in this respect low-income and/or first-generation college students start out *ahead* in the game. The same is true in different ways for women and BIPOC scholars—their experiences give them added advantages when it comes to adopting an entrepreneurial approach toward scholarship.

What This Book Is Based on and How It Is Organized

While the ideas in this book are based partly on my own experience in academia, I wanted to reach as broad a spectrum of scholars as I could, so I conducted extensive (1+ hour) interviews in-person or over Zoom between May 2022 and May 2023 with forty-three individuals across a range of disciplines, departments, ranks, and institutions. This was by no means a random or representative sample, and readers will notice that perspectives from the social sciences and humanities are overrepresented, while those from STEM fields are underrepresented. To get perspectives beyond my own social network, I asked people on different professional LISTSERVs to nominate scholars who they considered to be entrepreneurial. I also recruited some people by listening to podcasts about them and asking them for an interview. All but four interviewees have a PhD, but tellingly not all work in academia.

As a sociologist who studies inequality, it was especially important for me that readers who are women, FLI, or BIPOC see themselves in the examples shared in this book. About half of my sample identify as women, one-quarter BIPOC, and one-third FLI. All the people interviewed for this book gave me permission to use their real name when quoting them (see Table 1 at the end of the book) Please note that the titles and institutional affiliations mentioned reflect their status as of spring 2023 and may have changed since then.

In addition to interviews, I also draw on ideas from academic career guides,[35] entrepreneurship literature, and hundreds of hours of podcasts with academics (such as Steve Levitt's podcast, *People I Mostly Admire*), or podcasts targeted toward PhD students (e.g., *Hello PhD* targeted toward scientists). Finally, for the past four years, I have been running a fellowship program for students pursuing doctorates in education across universities in the United States, Canada and Israel. I have mentored sixteen students, most of whom wrote their dissertations while working part- or full-time.

This book unfolds in two parts. In the first part, I map out what I call an entrepreneurial mindset. Chapter 1 argues for the value of taking charge of your scholarship by adopting an entrepreneurial mindset. This entails rethinking your approach to your good student tendencies, believing in your ability to succeed, and taking ownership of your education and career. Chapter 2 describes the flip side of the entrepreneurial mindset that recognizes there are things you can't control. It examines how then to embrace unpredictability and still recognize you have options. Once the entrepreneurial mindset is in place, I then pivot to look at how to apply it in practice. Chapter 3 describes how to think of yourself as a knowledge producer in the idea business—to think about your work in terms of problems rather than topics and why it is important to solve problems that matter to you and the world. Chapter 4 argues that academics need to embrace relationship building and view academia as a team sport. It also outlines ideas for working with limited resources and financing your research through side jobs, grants, and fellowships. Chapter 5 talks about how to get your ideas "out there" both in and beyond the academy and provides ideas for what that could look like. I conclude with a final story about one early career scholar whose entrepreneurial mindset helped him become one of the most prolific scholars in his field, disseminating his ideas far beyond academia.

By the end of this book, I hope you feel more empowered to take charge of your educational and professional journey. By embracing the constraints of limited resources amid uncertain circumstances, I hope you come to see yourself as an entrepreneurial scholar—someone with the power to shape how people think, by producing knowledge and putting your ideas out into the world.

1

An Entrepreneurial Mindset

SARA BLAKELY WAS a twenty-seven-year-old graduate from Florida State when she was selling fax machines door-to-door in Clearwater, Florida in 1998. Blakely was good at her job, but she wasn't passionate about selling clunky office equipment in subtropical heat. Having failed the LSAT twice, she began listing her ambitions in a journal, where she wrote "I want to invent a product that I can sell to millions of people that will make them feel good."

One night soon thereafter she had a revelation. Blakely owned a pair of white pants she'd never worn because she didn't have any underwear that wouldn't show through the light fabric. She grabbed a pair of control-top pantyhose and cut off the feet. Though the edges of the hastily altered tights rolled up her legs, she was sure that the smoothed-out lineless look she'd achieved was something other women would happily pay for. With no formal design background or knowledge of how to start a business and just $5,000 in savings, Blakely began spending her nights and weekends doing research, going to fabric stores, assembling and testing prototypes, and even writing much of her own patent application.

The company that resulted from that idea, Spanx, now offers more than two hundred products in shapewear and other fashion categories. Its annual sales have been estimated at $400 million, making Blakely the youngest self-made female billionaire in the US. While the brilliance of Spanx now seems obvious, it took Blakely two years to get anyone to see the value of her idea, including family and friends. "When I chose to tell everybody, I was a year into the process. And I did hear things that, if I had heard them the first day I had the idea, I may have just stopped and would probably still be selling fax machines today," she says. She remembers being asked, "Sweetie, if it's such a good idea, why hasn't somebody else done it?" Others warned, "Even if this is a good idea, you're gonna spend your savings on it and the big guys will just knock you off six months later and you'll be done." Blakely was certainly rattled by the skepticism. "I think anybody who's doing something or creating something has a lot of inner dialogue about it already. So, there were bouts of serious self-doubt and conversations that I would have with myself, like, 'Is this really a crazy idea? What am I doing?'"[1] But she kept going.

When Blakely started investigating how she could get her product manufactured, she realized that most of America's hosiery was designed and manufactured in mills owned by men. She discovered that existing tights on the market were only tested on mannequins and not actual women with real skin that sweats. Learning this "actually energized me even more. Because once I saw how little attention was being paid to how we felt in the garments, I kind of became a crusader in my desire to really show the industry that we could make things so much better for women with just a little bit of extra love and care and attention."[2]

Eventually, one of the manufacturers—at the behest of his three daughters, who thought Spanx were a great idea—agreed to produce a batch. Blakely managed to find one Dallas-based Neiman Marcus buyer who agreed to talk. The buyer couldn't quite grasp the concept, so Blakely stopped the meeting and took the buyer into the bathroom. She proceeded to model the white pants with and without the Spanx. Then it clicked. "I get it!" the buyer said, and placed orders for seven stores. A few months later, Blakely appeared on Oprah Winfrey's "favorite things" episode, after Oprah's assistant passed her a pair of Spanx that Blakely had sent to the show.

Blakely's story is a "fitting" place to start because it reveals what it means to have an entrepreneurial *mindset*. A mindset refers to a network of interrelated cognitive beliefs that consist of assumptions, knowledge, and convictions. These elements assist us in interpreting information, directing our actions, and shaping our judgments. Mindsets are not fixed personality traits; they are malleable and can be developed over time. Your mindset is the bedrock of your behavior. Research in the psychology of entrepreneurship has shown that qualities like self-efficacy, autonomy, and creativity are closely linked to the ability to spot and seize opportunities.[3]

This chapter zeroes in on elements of the entrepreneurial mindset that are within your grasp. It's about recognizing that the traits of a good student are not the same as those required to excel as a scholar. It's about having faith in your capabilities when faced with obstacles and taking charge of your education and career. Although nurturing this facet of the entrepreneurial mindset might seem intimidating, the following pages will demonstrate that it's not only essential but also achievable for academics at any stage in their career to embrace this perspective.

Good Student versus Good Scholar

Many people enter grad school because they have a long track record of strong test scores and academic achievement. They have spent their life being praised for their intelligence, and probably expect that they'll do well in a PhD program. Joseph Conley, a former doctoral student who wrote publicly about his decision to leave his PhD, described how school was the only thing he knew how to do: "All of my training up to that point had made me exceptionally proficient at being a student, so jumping through the hoops required to get into a PhD program was right in my wheelhouse."[4] But when jumping through hoops turned into headstands and cartwheels, Conley found himself unprepared for the demands of academic research.

This focus on traditional measures of academic excellence is often especially pronounced among first-generation and/or low-income students. In a conversation on the podcast *Your Shadow Advisor*, Darrel Wanzer and Shantel Martinez, both of whom were the first in their families to attend college, describe their parents' intense focus on the traditional measures of academic excellence. Any deviation from a single-minded focus on grades, including participating in extracurricular activities, is oftentimes seen as incredibly risky. And yet the real risk is that in focusing exclusively on the "regurgitation" skills of traditional academics, students don't learn the deeper skill of creative thinking.

It's true that doctoral admissions committees often favor students who excel in traditional academic metrics. In her book on graduate student admissions, Julie Posselt, a professor of higher education at the USC School of Education, highlights the challenges faculty on admissions committees face in assessing a candidate's potential as a researcher. While they seek signs of intellectual curiosity, such evidence can be elusive, leading many faculty members to choose candidates who resemble their own academic profiles, often marked by high test scores and stellar grades.

The challenge is that experimenting with new criteria for evaluating candidates is easier said than done. Faculty members, burdened with the task of sifting through hundreds of applications, naturally gravitate toward familiar metrics like GRE scores and GPA to streamline the process and reduce conflict.[5] These measures are indeed linked to academic ability, but they don't necessarily equate to a candidate's capacity for generating new knowledge. This reliance on conventional metrics highlights a tension between the desire for innovation in admissions criteria and the practical constraints faced by faculty in the selection process.

It turns out that mere intelligence and high test scores are not enough to ensure success in academia. In his book *Behind the Academic Curtain*, Frank Furstenberg suggests that successful academics require a mindset that goes beyond the traditional skills rewarded in school. While doing well as an undergraduate is often necessary to enter a PhD program, it doesn't automatically make one suitable for a PhD. Students need to develop or possess a range of soft skills that complement their intellectual abilities. These include the ability to work independently, effectively utilize constructive feedback, multitask efficiently, overcome challenges, and stay focused despite external distractions.[6]

Most grad students have thrived within the structures of formal schooling that have brought them there. But traditional schooling is highly predictable because there is a script to schooling. This script is often referred to as the "hidden curriculum" of school, which entails the unofficial "three Rs"— rules, routines, and regulations.[7] These three Rs have to be learned by students to survive and thrive in classrooms. The hidden curriculum entails teaching kids to "fit in" with a social system, follow rules and order, respect authority, obey, compete, and achieve success within the boundaries of the system.[8] Those who figure out how to thrive based on that script are at the top of the educational ladder. In fact, they are so good at school that many choose to "go pro" by entering academia.

While being an excellent student is a prerequisite for getting into grad school, the skills that contribute to academic success are not the same as those required to produce original scholarship. Steve Levitt, an economist at the University of Chicago and coauthor of the bestselling book *Freakonomics*, likes to tell a story about when he first realized the difference between being good at school and being good at thinking. Levitt was an excellent student in high school and college, but it wasn't until his first day on the job in management consulting that the distinction between excelling academically and excelling in critical thinking was highlighted for him. His boss gave him a stack of documents that had some numbers about new drug applications to the FDA, and said to Levitt, "By the end of the week, I want you to tell me how our client can get their drugs approved faster." Levitt replied by saying that he didn't know anything about the FDA and asked how to do the task. He remembers his boss looking at him and saying, "Look, we're not paying you to tell you the answers." Levitt recalls breaking out in a cold sweat: "It was the first time, really, that anyone had asked me to think rather than to regurgitate. But what I realized is that I love to think. And I had never taken the luxury of thinking because it didn't serve me, because thinking wasn't helpful for getting an A. Regurgitation is what you needed to do."[9]

David Labaree, emeritus professor of education at Stanford, has worked with dozens of graduate students over the course of his career. Like Levitt, he argues that *thinking* is the most important skill that scholars have to cultivate to be successful: "The skills that get us *to* graduate school are not the ones we really use *in* graduate school. In graduate school, you've got to stop reading every page of every book and look for the stuff you want and push the other stuff aside. You've got to keep prioritizing around your own agenda instead of a course syllabus, program or advisors. That's hard for people who've always been good students. It's a hustle and people aren't prepared for that."

Because the script of schooling is so well-established and routinely followed, PhD students likely see themselves as being in the passenger's seat of their education rather than in the driver's seat. As Steven Zhou, a PhD student at George Mason University, puts it, "There is a huge misunderstanding where people think that to get a PhD, I'm going to follow this curriculum, check these boxes, and I'll be good to go. And I always want to warn them: when you move into the PhD, it's not like that. You'll have some benchmarks along the way, and hopefully you have helpful advisors, but they're not going to tell you what to do. They are going to wait for you to ask them for help."

Many doctoral programs fail to emphasize that the world of academia actually prioritizes knowledge production (i.e., thinking) over knowledge consumption. They don't tell their students that they need to fundamentally reimagine what it takes to succeed in the academy. This early disconnect sets doctoral students down a confusing and lonely path through graduate school, where once you get past your initial exams (sometimes called comps), there's this kind of emptiness.[10] It's just you and the books. There is no regular method of support.

This problem isn't unique to graduate students. The same issues plague professors as well. Matt Welsh, a former computer science professor, notes that although a PhD program is less structured than school, there's still plenty of ways to do well just by following all the rules. "I saw plenty of 'successful PhD students'—the ones that crank out the most papers who've basically learned the formula for how you write a paper that is going to get into the right conferences/journal and you get a CV with all the publications on it." But there's just one problem. "Now you're a professor and you're like, oh, I've got to actually create something that's my brand. I've got to create an organization around these ideas that I want to pursue." To be sure, some of the people who have been the rule followers can still do that as a professor, but they tend to be followers rather than leaders and work on established problems identified in other people's work. "They're not the trailblazers—they're not the ones creating new domains or new areas of research. They're just contributors . . . and they just keep playing that game over and over." There's little chance that such scholars will move up the academic ladder or even achieve tenure.

Being good at school has created in many academics the constant need to show that we know the right answer. But that approach has inhibited their entrepreneurial mindset and resulted in roadblocks to academic success. Here's what to do about it.

Celebrating Autonomy

Paige Harden, a professor of psychology at UT Austin, champions the idea of graduate students setting their own goals. Her love for academia stems from the autonomy it provides: the freedom to decide what to do, how to do it, and when to do it. This autonomy was a revelation for Harden, who realized after being fired from retail jobs that she wanted to be her own boss. Graduate school and an academic career provided the perfect environment for her to exercise this autonomy, enabling her to be productive on her own terms.

Autonomy is a cornerstone of the entrepreneurial mindset. Entrepreneurs are self-starters, driven by their own initiatives rather than external pressures. Harden encourages her graduate students to adopt this mindset, emphasizing that they are responsible for driving their education and research. While advisors can offer guidance, the ultimate responsibility for setting goals and making progress lies with the students themselves. As Harden puts it: "Advisors do not bear the responsibility of your outcome of grad school. They give you space and some money so that you don't starve, but you have to figure things out." There are some things that advisors are well-positioned to do, such as suggest things to read, but it is up to the student to do the readings and then figure out how they help advance their own thinking. "I set my goals," says Harden. "If I don't have anything to show for my efforts, that's on me—not my advisors."

Entrepreneurial scholars like Harden are deeply motivated by autonomy—the feeling that their actions are the result of their own choices and decisions and not the result of external pressures.[11] They want to be in control of their own destiny, make decisions that align with their personal values and vision, and be able to take risks without being constrained by the demands of others. Psychologists Richard Ryan and Edward Deci identified autonomy as one of the three basic psychological needs that lead to motivation. This desire for autonomy is often what *drives* entrepreneurs to start their own businesses, as it allows them to be in charge of their own success and create something that is a reflection of their own values and identity. Entrepreneurs tend to be people who feel their autonomy is undermined by following processes that other people have created, especially if those processes don't make sense to them. They want to establish the rules and workflows that make sense for what they are doing without relying on others to motivate them.

For all its faults, academia offers a lot of autonomy and opportunities to practice entrepreneurial thinking. Michael Weisbach, author of *The Economist's Craft*, puts it like this: "If you are like 99 percent of people on this planet, being told to 'go to your office and think up something great' is a paralyzing and terrifying mandate . . . [But] academic research is liberating. You have time to pursue ideas of your own choosing."[12] Harden tries to impress this onto her graduate students. She wants people to think intentionally about how they can use this time to cultivate marketable skills and determine what will distinguish them from others: "The mindset of academia is not sealed off from creating human capital and marketing how we are valuable to other people. It's core to what we do." Think of these skills as tools of the trade that go beyond the ivory tower: data analysis that can crack open mysteries in any field, project management that keeps the gears of industry turning, and writing that can persuade even the toughest critics. The message is clear: academics need to think about how they can create opportunities for themselves. They should not wait for their advisors or academia to create opportunities for them. You're not just preparing for a life in academia; you're gearing up for a world of possibilities. The question is not just "What do I know?" but "What can I do with what I know?"

This proactive mindset is especially crucial for underrepresented minorities and FLI students, who may have grown up in cultures with more hierarchical structures that encourage deference to faculty. Advocating for yourself becomes vital in navigating these dynamics. Ideally, your relationship with your advisor should be a partnership rather than an employer/employee relationship, and your needs should be prioritized, not the faculty's research. Advisors should continue to play crucial roles in students' graduate education, but as Leonard Cassuto observes, they should be "an organizing point person, rather than a directing force."[13] Advisors should empower their advisees rather than dictate to them the direction of their research. "Your advisors can help you steer," he says, "but you have to set the direction."[14] However, the reality of academia might not always align with this ideal. Many doctoral students find themselves constrained by advisors who expect them to prioritize faculty interests over their own. When selecting an advisor, look for someone who respects your autonomy and supports your pursuit of independent ideas.

Howard Gardner's unconventional academic journey exemplifies the power of autonomy. When Howard Gardner received a MacArthur Fellowship in 1981 for his research on how intelligence works, he wasn't working as a professor. In fact, since receiving his PhD in developmental psychology from Harvard a decade earlier, Gardner had been raising money to pursue his research outside the traditional tenure-track path. It wasn't until the mid-1980s—about fifteen years after completing his PhD—that Gardner finally received a faculty position. But taking an unconventional route through academia didn't deter Gardner, nor hinder his productivity. Before being offered a tenure-track position, Gardner managed to publish seven books and over a hundred scholarly articles.

Although Gardner found his undergraduate years to be deeply stimulating, he hated graduate school.[15] Several aspects troubled him: he felt disconnected from many of his classmates and key faculty, preferred thinking broadly but found it difficult to stay within the confines of experimental psychology, and struggled with the hierarchical nature of graduate school, where students were often expected to carry out their advisors' work. As he put it, he didn't want to be "disciplined by the discipline"—he envisioned an exploratory journey, synthesizing knowledge broadly in one area before moving on to a different topic.

After weighing the pros and cons of continuing his PhD, Gardner made a decision: he would finish his degree as long as he could do what he wanted to do in the way he wanted to do it. Once he made this decision, Gardner decided he would ignore the things that didn't work for him and the people who he didn't get along with and instead just take advantage of the things he did enjoy, even though he didn't yet know what that would look like.[16]

To continue his PhD the way he wanted to, Gardner would have to operate more autonomously than the average student in his program. For example, graduate students who worked in one psychology lab were discouraged, if not forbidden, from working in other labs, (this was in the 1960s so norms may have evolved since then). So Gardner decided not to join a lab. Since he was not working under the supervision of a faculty member, he had to figure things out for himself. But not joining a lab gave him more freedom to pursue his own intellectual curiosities. "Years later, I observed that the students who landed the best initial jobs were ones who had been the best widgets as doctoral students, but in most cases not the ones who ultimately went on to change the field or the conversation. Being a widget does not easily translate into being a wizard."[17]

Relationship building, a crucial skill for entrepreneurs, was also crucial for Gardner. Since he wasn't part of a lab, Gardner sought out several mentors who supported his work and whom he could learn from. "You should take skills and traits from different mentors. Don't have your dissertation advisor as the be all end all," he told me. He describes this as "frag-mentoring": the opportunity to emulate particular aspects of particular mentors. Faculty have different skills and time constraints, and having a team of mentors allows you to leverage their expertise and availability. Having a team of mentors can also help attenuate your fear that they will judge you negatively, because you can share different kinds of problems with different mentors.[18]

Gardner also feels strongly about cultivating relationships—with postdocs, research assistants, and coauthors: "I think the most successful academic entrepreneurs are people who are leaders in the sense that they inspire people to want to work with them." He keeps in touch with all sorts of people, even funders who turned him down: "It's never a mistake to keep in touch because the very person who's turned you down three times might reach out to you when something new comes up. I look at it as promising soil where you can do something that people find interesting and useful at the right time."

Gardner was also entrepreneurial in how he pursued directions that he didn't anticipate. "I didn't worry about failing. I allowed my curiosity and the questions I was posing myself to proceed in new and unanticipated directions." One day while taking a class in grad school, his professor mentioned that Nelson Goodman, then a professor at Brandeis, was considering coming to Harvard to start a research project in the arts and was looking for research assistants (RAs). Gardner reached out to Goodman and was soon interviewing with him. Goodman ended up founding Project Zero, and Gardner was one of the first RAs. After Goodman left, Gardner took over running Project Zero, and has done so for fifty-five years, raising millions of dollars along the way. Project Zero is a research center at Harvard that initially focused on understanding learning through the arts. It has since expanded its mission to explore and nurture human potentials—such as learning, thinking, ethics, intelligence, and creativity—in all individuals.

Navigating Self-Doubt with Confidence

Shantel Martinez, a first-generation college student who earned a PhD in communications and media studies, describes her PhD experience as "walking at night on a path in a dense forest during a new moon, where you stumble and can't see the tree roots in front of you. You have to pick yourself up and have faith that you're moving forward on this pathway, even if you can't see it."[19] Shantel Martinez's description of her PhD experience illustrates the challenges of academic uncertainty. However, many PhD students and academics at all stages struggle with self-doubt, often exacerbated by impostor syndrome.

Impostor syndrome is characterized by low self-confidence, difficulty in realistically assessing one's competence and skills, attributing success to external factors, berating performance regardless of outcomes, fearing unmet expectations, and significant self-doubt.[20] Impostor syndrome often leads to individuals internally feeling like "a fraud" or "a phony" and doubting their abilities. They harbor the belief that they do not "measure up" to expectations, resulting in feelings of anxiety about being "found out"—despite oftentimes being high-performing individuals. It is especially common among women, People of Color, and people from lower-income backgrounds.[21]

Consider the career of Maureen Gannon. She finished her undergraduate training in just three years, had a full scholarship to pursue a master's degree, completed a PhD at Cornell, and is now a tenured faculty member at the School of Medicine at Vanderbilt University. She leads and chairs multiple organizations and committees and is invited to speak internationally about her work. By any reasonable measure she is a remarkably successful academic. And yet during much of her training, Maureen didn't feel successful. She would attribute her personal wins to outside forces or good luck and was constantly waiting for the moment when others would discover her shortcomings as a scientist. But then she attended a workshop that put a name to the feelings: *impostor syndrome.*

Alison Miller, who received her PhD in clinical psychology and then went on to start an organization that offers dissertation and thesis coaching to graduate students, sees impostor syndrome as a significant issue in academia: "The amount of fear in academia is inherently limiting the impact of these people who have chosen to carve out a path of engaging with ideas and concepts and theories and who do Olympic level intellectual work. Learning and doing research are vulnerable acts that require struggle, periods of confusion, and making mistakes. It is hard to learn well when you feel afraid . . . All this fear can cause academics to over-focus on protecting and surviving and under-focus on learning, growth, and what is possible."

I battled with impostor syndrome for the first few years of my PhD program. I didn't understand academic discourse. I remember the first time someone asked, "Who is this author in conversation with?" I was totally confused by the remark—what did the phrase even mean? "What is their scholarly intervention?" was another phrase that threw me. Then there were the dozens of "foreign" terms that baffled me: R&Rs, qualifying paper, job talks. I felt so lost that on several occasions I openly cried in my advisor's office.

The problem with impostor syndrome is that even the experience of doing well at something does nothing to change your beliefs. The thought still nags in your head, "What gives me the right to be here?" What's worse is that the more you accomplish, the more you feel like a fraud, as your successes are viewed as more evidence of your having "pulled the wool" over the eyes of others. Only you see matters "clearly," and as a result you can't internalize your experiences of success.[22] Acknowledging impostor syndrome is the first step toward overcoming it. By recognizing that these feelings are common among high achievers, you can begin to separate your self-worth from external validation and focus on your genuine capabilities and accomplishments.

To navigate this journey, you need a degree of confidence and belief in your abilities—what psychologists call self-efficacy.[23] Entrepreneurial self-efficacy is a belief that entrepreneurs have in their own ability to begin new ventures, but it applies to scholars as well. In the context of academia, this means having confidence in your capacity to succeed as a scholar, while remaining open to learning and growth.

The challenge is that rather than feeling a sense of self-efficacy, many PhD students (and successful academics at all stages of their careers) are plagued by a sense of doubt, regardless of how much success they have experienced.[24] Self-efficacy is not about never doubting yourself, but about having the resilience to keep moving forward despite those doubts. This requires understanding academia's hierarchical nature. Graduate students are on the bottom rung of a very tall ladder, aspiring to know as much as their advisors who tower over them at the top. As my former colleague Tamara Gilkes Borr describes, in academia you're mostly just doing what the professor or PI (principal investigator) told you to do. You might have a good idea, but they probably already thought of it because they are the subject matter expert, so you don't have as many eureka moments where your professor is like, "wow, that was a fantastic idea." Borr, who worked as a consultant after her PhD, observed that other industries are not as hierarchical: "In business and journalism, you work in teams and ideas flow in several directions. But in academia, they seemed to flow in one direction. In my job at Boston Consulting Group (BCG) or at *The Economist*, after a few times of presenting something to a senior person and having your idea get accepted, you start to view yourself as somebody who can have great ideas."

Borr felt a profound sense of insecurity about her abilities during grad school. If she could go back in time, she would change her mindset. For example, when she first learned about a summer job at The College Board (the organization in charge of AP and SAT exams), she thought she was totally underqualified. "I never thought I would get it, but I did." As she recalls:

> If PhDs could just get rid of the inner critic . . . we are so down on ourselves about being worthless. I just spent so many years staring at my blank CV. I was sad about it every

day . . . I remember in grad school just sitting around waiting for someone to tell me I was good at what I was doing.

Borr didn't realize how insecure she had become until she
went to work at BCG after her PhD. "At BCG, everybody just
knew they were good, even though no one was telling them
that. And it was just amazing—they had so much confidence,"
she told me. Why was that the case, and what can graduate
students do about it? "You gotta get yourself out of that space,
whether it's speaking to family members, therapy, internships,
whatever you need—to remember your value."

Moving forward despite self-doubt can be especially difficult
when other people underestimate you and question your place
in academia. Research shows that scholars of color, especially
women, have long experienced bias and discrimination in academia.[25] Several people I interviewed know this feeling all too
well. When I spoke with Narketta Sparkman-Key, the Vice Provost for Strategic Initiatives and Global Affairs at James Madison University, she told me about a lunch she had volunteered
to attend with the then-current dean of Old Dominion University, where she had landed her first tenure-track position. When
she arrived at the lunch, she noticed that she was the only person of color, and one of the first questions she was asked was,
"So how long have you been a student here?" Key didn't look
especially young, but the faculty member's image of a professor
was probably not one of a Black woman: "The assumption was
that people who look like me don't become professors."

For Key, this lunch was just one of many moments where
she felt like she didn't belong in academia. Her path had been
difficult from the start, making her question her abilities and

place in the academy at many points along the way. She had pursued her PhD as a single mother, taking classes through an online program with very little funding. Her sense of insecurity reached its peak during her third-year review as a faculty member when she was told that despite her ten publications and what she considered a strong record of teaching and service, she was not on track toward tenure and promotion.

Bogged down by a sense of impostor syndrome and stress, Key decided that checking the boxes that academia set for her was not going to be enough. "I didn't want to let higher education be the dictator of what my career should look like." She decided to take more ownership of her career and responsibility for the direction of her life.

Taking Ownership

What does it mean to own your journey—or what Key calls "bossing up"?[26] Owning your career does not mean taking on more work. It means committing to supporting and promoting yourself. Key's advice encompasses several important aspects for maintaining mental wellness and professional growth. These include creating a personal self-care strategy and seeking dependable allies, prioritizing factors within your control that can be altered, assuming responsibility for progress instead of relying on external validation, dispelling negative thoughts such as impostor syndrome, assuming control over professional development by identifying necessary skills and seeking opportunities to acquire them, embracing risks to foster personal growth, advocating for oneself, and pursuing roles that amplify individual strengths.

What did this process entail for Key? First, Key embarked on a journey to find her own voice and confront the emotional distress triggered by her performance review. She pursued a path of forgiveness while addressing the inaccuracies present in the review. Ultimately, the college committee reconsidered their decision and acknowledged that Key was indeed making progress toward tenure. Second, Key utilized her voice as a means to share her experiences and shed light on the marginalization that occurs within the tenure process. She established a support network outside her department, consisting of women who could provide nurturing guidance and mentorship. She also actively engaged in external networks specifically designed for women of color in academia, recognizing the significance of such networks (explored in greater detail in Chapter 4).

Third, Key formulated clear goals and devised a well-defined plan to achieve them. She identified the most suitable platforms for her research and focused on publishing her work through those channels. To prioritize research, Key limited her attendance at conferences to once a year. She also made a conscious decision to refrain from taking on additional teaching responsibilities, concentrating solely on the courses required of her each semester. Instead, she actively sought collaborations beyond her department, which injected fresh energy and innovative ideas into her research endeavors. Key also proactively approached her dean to discuss her career aspirations, ensuring that the dean remained aware of her desire for opportunities to develop the necessary skills for growth. As a result of these conversations, she was provided with the opportunity to attend leadership training for women. This experience propelled her into the roles of program director and assistant chair of her department. In taking responsibility for the direction of her life and her dreams, Key started to see her experience as a Black woman as an asset: "Now when I walk into spaces, I am confident about who I am because I recognize that no one in that space has what I can give and what I can bring."

Key also describes the importance of diversifying your source of joy by having projects outside academia. "My mind does not work in just one avenue. I need to have a creative aspect to me. I'm not predictable. Being entrepreneurial means having a mindset in which I can fulfill all my different interests in any way I'd like to. And that feels like freedom." Key also makes it a point to look inward and think about what she values most. "What brings me the most joy? What do I contribute? What is my purpose?" she asked herself. Being self-aware of what you need to thrive is crucial for recognizing your value, both personally and professionally. For Key, this meant recognizing the contributions she was making outside of academia: "My joy is wrapped up in a multitude of experiences and things. You need to focus on what brings you joy as opposed to what the system wants from you. It took a long time for me to feel valued by the academy, but I felt valued by other communities I was a part of."

David Zvi Kalman struggled throughout his PhD at the University of Pennsylvania in Jewish studies, partly because he went into the program as "the obvious next step for someone who was a good student." As someone with an academic parent, it seemed like a feasible career path. "I used to have the mindset that I needed to check as many boxes as possible. The way that you get ahead is by demonstrating that you're the smartest person in the room and that you can write amazing things. And if you do that, then you will naturally be recognized, and your applications will be selected. Within an academic context that can get you pretty far." But after having a child, Kalman felt himself floundering and he didn't feel motivated to keep going with his PhD. The strategy that he had used to excel in life was no longer working.

Struggling to write his dissertation, Kalman decided instead to start two companies. He eventually finished his PhD but resolved that the typical academic career was not for him. He still participates in academic conferences and writes for academic outlets, but he also works for a think tank and has several entrepreneurial ventures on the side. His ultimate realization was that he no longer wanted to check other people's boxes; he wanted to create his own: "Entrepreneurship requires a pretty significant shift in mindset. It requires saying like, no—you can make your own boxes . . . You can actually decide on your own terms what is valuable and build things that didn't exist before." Adopting an entrepreneurial mindset changes the game for how you look at yourself and your career path. "PhD programs don't give you a sense that you're supposed to be a leader, or that you're supposed to be in charge of the process. They give you a sense that there's this machine that you're a part of." But interestingly, both PhD programs and entrepreneurial settings leave you "to your own devices for a lot of time. It's a sink or swim mentality." The only real difference is in how you choose to conceive the endgame. "Are you just trying to get this piece of paper saying you have a doctorate? Or is it that you actually get to set your own goals about what matters?" Both are possible outcomes of graduate studies, but only one gives you a sense of ownership over the goals you set and the work you perform.

Kalman's remarks point to an important fact: no one is born with an entrepreneurial mindset. According to Rob Lalka—a professor at Tulane's Business School who also has been an entrepreneur, board director, diplomat, and venture capitalist at different points in his career—one of the most destructive myths that people tell themselves is that entrepreneurs always look like Mark Zuckerburg, Steve Jobs, and Bill Gates; that is, someone who drops out of college to start a business. "These men, who are thought to have some very special unique talent, are the heroes in this myth. But that is not reality. Entrepreneurship is simply about bringing creativity and ingenuity to problem-solving so that you can create something that didn't exist before or adapting something from a different area to a new application in a way that's really innovative."

Being entrepreneurial isn't an innate talent. It means taking responsibility for making things happen and not blaming circumstances. In the case of academics, that means not acting as if you are at the mercy of your environment. For graduate students, taking personal initiative means taking charge of one's academic path—no longer settling for the passenger seat but moving over to the driver seat and assuming control of your education and your career. I got my first taste of what that felt like during my fourth year of graduate school, when I realized that I wasn't going to be competitive on the academic job market. I didn't have enough publications for research universities, but I also didn't have enough teaching experience for teaching-focused institutions. I had never been the instructor of record for a course, and I didn't have any teaching evaluations. So I started exploring opportunities to get teaching experience by asking my classmates if they had any ideas. A few weeks later my talking paid off—one of my classmates was at church talking to a fellow congregant, the assistant dean at one of the local community colleges, and he happened to be looking for a sociology instructor. When she emailed me to tell me about her conversation, I jumped at the opportunity and contacted him immediately.

There was just one remaining hitch. I knew teaching my own course would be a great way to get experience, course evaluations, and make some extra money, but I also knew that it was going to be time consuming. After all, I was still taking courses and had a four-month-old baby and a four-year-old. So I came up with a plan to coteach the class with a colleague. I pitched this unconventional plan to the dean and department chair and they agreed. I taught the first half of the semester, and my colleague Diana taught the second half. We would both get the teaching experience, but with half the workload.

Why It Matters

Howard Gardner wasn't alone in recognizing that agency and an entrepreneurial mindset were key to successfully navigating academia, but he got there faster than most. It took Borr a long time to see that she needed to take more control of her future. She had spent six years as a graduate student, working nights and weekends toward her goal of becoming a professor, but constantly felt like she had nothing of value to offer her field. Reflecting on her situation, she realized that she lacked control and felt overreliant on her advisors, and as a result had an unhealthy sense of self. Borr realized she had to do something outside academia. When she received a job offer at BCG, several colleagues tried to convince her to stay in academia. "Everybody was telling me that all I need is a postdoc—just another couple of years. And I was like, not only was I not getting anywhere, but I wasn't getting anywhere because I wasn't exercising control. I was waiting for other people. I was waiting for advisors. Once I felt like I no longer had my destiny in my control, it was time to go."

Once she left academia, Borr finally felt like she had options. She recalls how liberating it felt when BCG asked her which three cities she most wanted to live in. "I had conditioned myself to think that I would live in the middle of nowhere to stay in academia and drag my fiancé around with me, but now I didn't have to make huge sacrifices for my career. BCG made me feel that I was valuable, and that my time was valuable. They made me feel that it was okay to prioritize myself." Borr's advice to scholars is this: "Don't be afraid to change career paths. Don't be afraid to do new things. Just always do something that opens doors rather than closes them. And don't feel like you're too old to start something new. I was thirty-five and I felt like I was too old to work in consulting. But I wasn't. You're not too old to take charge and try new things." Borr also advises people to advocate for themselves: "If you see something and you want it, you have to ask for it. You don't have to be aggressive, but you have to be your own advocate. The worst thing that can happen is somebody says no. That's something that I saw a lot of my colleagues at BCG and even here at *The Economist*—they ask for things they want. But I didn't see a lot of that among people in academia."

When cultivating an entrepreneurial mindset, remember that the transition from being a successful student to becoming a successful scholar requires a significant shift in perspective. Here are the key points to keep in mind:

Move from good student to good scholar: The leap from excelling in structured educational environments to thriving in the less predictable realm of academic research demands a reevaluation of what success means. You are no longer just a consumer of knowledge but a producer of original ideas.

Celebrate autonomy: An entrepreneurial scholar celebrates the autonomy that academia offers. This freedom to pursue your passions and interests is a privilege that should be leveraged to its fullest potential. Use this autonomy to carve out a unique path that aligns with your values and goals, and in doing so, make a lasting impact on your field and beyond.

Navigate self-doubt with confidence: Central to this entrepreneurial mindset is a strong sense of self-efficacy. You must trust in your capabilities to overcome challenges and achieve your goals, even when faced with skepticism or setbacks. Believing in yourself propels you forward so that you can tackle ambitious projects and contribute meaningfully to your field.

Take ownership: Embracing an entrepreneurial mindset also means taking control of your academic journey. It's about setting your agenda, defining your success metrics, and actively seeking opportunities to grow and learn. Be proactive in your research, seek out mentors and collaborators, and take charge of your professional development.

2

Navigating Uncertainty

IN THE PREVIOUS chapter, we explored the aspects of the entrepreneurial mindset that you can control, such as embracing the production of knowledge, cultivating a success-oriented attitude, and taking ownership of your actions. Now, in Chapter 2, we turn our attention to navigating the unpredictable and uncertain elements of academia and beyond.

Jennifer Burns was a graduate student in the history department at UC Berkeley, where she wrote a paper on Ayn Rand. While researching the topic, Burns noticed that no scholars in her field of American intellectual history had written a peer-reviewed article or book on Rand, and that all existing writings about her were authored by either Rand's allies or adversaries. This realization prompted Burns to question the lack of critical academic attention that other contemporary novelists had received. By utilizing her previous knowledge of the literature, Burns recognized an unaddressed niche in the market. She realized that to conduct the kind of research that would generate innovative ideas and contribute significantly to scholarship, she would need to delve into the original sources generated by Ayn Rand herself.

While searching for ways to obtain access to Rand's documents, Burns recognized an opportunity. The Ayn Rand Institute (ARI) had recently announced the creation of an archive. Although not yet open to the public, there was a newsletter, which Burns took as a sign that they might be interested in visitors. Burns inquired and was surprised when she was permitted to access the archive with one caveat: she could not utilize the material to create a biography, as the Ayn Rand Institute had already commissioned one. Since Burns was interested in Rand from the perspective of an intellectual historian and not a biographer, this stipulation was not an issue.

During her eight years spending time in the archives, Burns's project was fraught with uncertainty and risk. She was concerned that ARI might revoke her access since she was delving into Rand's personal artifacts. Moreover, Burns worried about how the ARI staff would perceive her critical stance on Rand. Another risk was whether she would be able to publish her research. Burns needed permission from the estate to use excerpts from Rand's unpublished writings. When Burns finally secured permission for all but two quotes, it was the first time Rand's estate had allowed an outside scholar to publish a full-length critical study of the author. Despite the risk that her work would never see the light of day, Burns persevered, and her book, *Goddess of the Market: Ayn Rand and the American Right*,[1] wound up having a significant impact among scholars and the general public, becoming Bloomberg News' 2009 top nonfiction book of the year, and even leading to Burns appearing on *The Colbert Report* and *The Daily Show*.

Tricia Bruce also faced a lot of risk and uncertainty when she left her tenured position in a sociology department at a small liberal arts college to create her own path in academia that allowed her to focus on research, writing, and public-facing work. Bruce started her academic career on the standard trajectory, but she was bothered by the way the academy drew boundary lines about what counts as academic scholarship and what doesn't. In particular, she was frustrated that the academy doesn't encourage scholars to collaborate and communicate across audiences. "It's a rather radical idea for an academic to believe that their ideas can make a difference in the world. Because we're trained to produce ideas that become publications and lines on your CV, that gives you jobs and promotions. There is certainly value in that, but we often forget to ask ourselves why we're doing what we're doing, or what difference it's making, or how it translates into a broader social understanding that could actually shift people's views and begin to change not only how we understand society, but what society is. To me, that was so compelling that I realized I had to make a fairly dramatic change in my own career trajectory."

Bruce wanted to pursue projects that she thought mattered to the world beyond the academy rather than abiding by the standard measures of success in academia such as citation counts. Her spouse, an entrepreneur, encouraged her: "If there isn't some structure for you, then you build it." So Bruce decided that the best way to pursue her work in the way she wanted and to have it inform real-world debates was to leave her tenured position. "I wanted to take on an entrepreneurial lifestyle and do this differently than the 'academic' world as we have defined it. There are different ways to fashion an academic life of thinking, research, and writing that are not confined to typical university jobs. So I left and redefined myself in a new space."

To navigate this new world outside the traditional tenure track, Bruce had to change how she thought about herself. Her established networks and reputation helped secure an affiliation with a university, and she started calling herself a sociologist and an author rather than a professor. But it took confidence. "It's exciting and unpredictable. Leaving the tenure track is not for those who need a high level of assurance and stability, because I don't know what every year looks like. But I'm confident in myself and know that I can figure it out. There's so much more that I want to do and build. I wake up knowing that I control my life and my day."

Bruce also points out that your reputation is based on the quality of your work: "You have to stand by your work, and you have to do good work, especially when you don't have the institutional title that may substitute or serve as a proxy for an evaluation of your work. Your reputation stands on who you are and what you produce." Being an entrepreneurial scholar has not prevented Bruce from holding leadership positions in key professional organizations: she currently serves as chair of the American Sociological Association Religion Section as well as a council member and president-elect for the Association for the Sociology of Religion. She is also the author of several books with top presses and makes regular media appearances to discuss religion, political attitudes, religious organizations, and social change.

The world is an unpredictable place, but scholars still have a choice whether to resign themselves to unpredictability or embrace it by "failing forward" and learning from one's mistakes (instead of running from them like "good" students do). In the challenging environment of higher education, you may even consider careers beyond academia. If honing the skills to manage what you can control, as discussed in Chapter 1, is challenging, then developing the abilities to navigate uncertainty and embrace what you can't control is even more demanding. However, developing these aspects of the entrepreneurial mindset is crucial for confronting the challenges of academia. While you may not emerge unscathed, you will gain the resources and attitudes necessary to succeed on your own terms.

The Unpredictability of Academia

PhD programs don't come with a warning label, but they should. They require a high tolerance for uncertainty, ambiguity, and risk. After all, academia is all about discovery, and discovery is inherently unpredictable. Just consider that only about 50 percent of students complete their doctoral degree.[2] Unlike professional programs like law or medicine, where graduation is almost a given, PhD programs offer no such guarantees. As Dalton Conley, a sociology professor, once said, "There's no structure. You have an enormous amount of freedom, and that's scary."

The uncertainty only grows when you dive into the research. Will your experiment work? Will enough people participate in your study? Will you get access to the archives or data you need? It's a roller coaster of "what ifs."

The uncertainties of a PhD program are compounded by the life changes and demands that often occur during this stage.

This is typically a time for forging romantic relationships, achieving financial stability, buying a home, and starting a family, all of which add complexity and pressure to the PhD journey. Making plans becomes exceedingly difficult when you're unsure of how long you'll live in your current location, where you'll move next, and how much that new location will cost. Many couples find their relationships strained by the nebulous nature of the PhD and the uncertainty of life afterward.

And the uncertainty doesn't end with obtaining a PhD—there's the job search, which is far from guaranteed, and then the climb up the academic ladder to tenure. Scholars often struggle to cope with the high level of uncertainty in academia.

This is where adopting an entrepreneurial mindset can be transformative. Entrepreneurs thrive in uncertain environments by being flexible and adaptable, using available resources to create new opportunities. Saras Sarasvathy calls this "effectuation"—instead of trying to predict the future, you focus on what you can do now with the resources you have.[3] With effectual thinking, surprises are viewed as possible opportunities rather than problems. Instead of starting with a specific goal and then seeking the means to achieve it, effectuation begins with the means at hand and allows goals to emerge over time. The guiding question is, "Given who I am, what I know, and who I know, what kind of opportunities could I create?"

For my parents, this approach meant leveraging their engineering and design expertise, along with their connections to other Russian speakers in the Philadelphia area, to create opportunities in home renovation and rental businesses. When I was a teenager, I often accompanied my mom to work. This meant going into whatever dilapidated house she bought and was in the process of renovating. I remember a home she was particularly excited about, but when I walked in, I couldn't understand why. All I could see were faults—the pee stains on the carpet, the grime on the tiles, the mold on the walls. It was *gross*. My mom, on the other hand, saw all its potential. She told me that if all I see is darkness and despair, that's all there's ever going to be. But if I could learn to see the beauty and warmth that this house could have for a family one day, then I could make the home different. She taught me that it is this inner capacity to choose our attitude in a situation that makes all the difference.[4] This spirit is what made her such an amazing entrepreneur—she dealt with problems by turning them into opportunities.

The entrepreneurial spirit my mother embodied—turning challenges into opportunities—was a lesson that stayed with me. Years later, I found myself facing my own set of challenges during the spring and summer of 2020. My initial plan to dedicate these months to writing my first book was completely upended. Confined to a small apartment with my young daughters and with my husband busier than ever, I was overwhelmed. At the same time, I was aware of how the pandemic was impacting college students, particularly those who relied on work-study jobs.

That's when I saw a chance to turn two problems into an opportunity. I needed help, and the students needed income. Although I was just a postdoc and couldn't directly hire work-study students, I reached out to my graduate school advisor for assistance. He was initially skeptical but agreed to sign off on the paperwork. From April to June 2020, I hired several work-study students who significantly advanced my research.

The solution that I thought was temporary lasted even longer. By early June, many students had lost their summer internships due to ongoing lockdowns. The students I hired were benefiting so much from the experience that they asked to stay on for the summer. I brought in another faculty member to help manage the additional hires. In total, I had eighteen students working for me full-time throughout the summer.

These students were not only earning an income but also gaining valuable research experience. They played a central role in analyzing data for two of my projects, and several even coauthored papers with me. I organized a reading curriculum focused on diversity, equity, and inclusion, and arranged for the authors of each book to engage with the students via Zoom. This experience was so impactful that several students went on to pursue social science majors and original research agendas.

Just like improvisational comedians, who build stories on the fly by responding to their partners and the audience, scholars can benefit from being open to different directions and possibilities. Effectual thinking in research means leveraging your resources to generate new ideas and approaches, viewing surprises as opportunities for learning and innovation. It's about taking risks and being willing to pivot your research direction if necessary.

Historically, US universities have provided a secure environment for intellectual exploration, with federal, state, and corporate funding supporting it. However, in today's climate, there is a shift away from exploratory research, with all parties involved preferring sure bets. Most of the funding is allocated to ideas and techniques that have already proven profitable in the past, and it's increasingly difficult to get nonmainstream ideas accepted by peer review, supported by universities, or financed by grant agencies.[5] But as Angus Fletcher, a professor of story science at the Ohio State University puts it, "Creativity isn't about guessing the future correctly. It's about making yourself open to imagining radically different possibilities."[6]

Susan Athey is a great example of what it looks like to have the courage to invent your own path. In 2007, Athey was working as a professor of economics and business when she received an unexpected phone call: Steve Ballmer, then the CEO of Microsoft, wanted to meet with her. Ballmer had read an article about Athey which highlighted her expertise in auctions. At the time, Microsoft was struggling to compete with Google, especially their use of auctions for advertising, and Ballmer wanted Athey to provide some fresh thinking on the problem. For Athey, this was a risky move. Ballmer's ask was incredibly open-ended, and she had never consulted for a company. At that time, leaving academia to work for a private company was uncommon.[7]

But as Athey thought more about the opportunity, she was intrigued by the problems she could explore at Microsoft. Athey already knew that digitization and tech platforms were going to play a significant role in the economy,[8] and that search engines were poised to have outsized importance. She also knew that the research community was just beginning to tackle questions about how to design digital markets and what healthy competition looked like in those markets, and she was excited to help develop that research. She decided the risk was worth the reward.

At Microsoft, Athey saw an opportunity to combine the computational advances from predictive machine learning with statistical theory so that researchers could better understand causal effects not only in business applications like the search engine but also in social science and economics. The creators of the Bing search engine were conducting experiments in a manner that economists only dreamed about. They were simultaneously running thousands of randomized A/B tests—asking large numbers of "what if" questions to better understand such things as which search results should rise to the top and how to run auctions for setting advertising prices on a search page. By comparison, economists typically run one experiment in a year. She recalls being totally overwhelmed by realizing the plethora of important implications she saw, none of which academia had recognized based on the scale and scope of the data they used: "Most academics didn't even understand what these problems were. I was familiarizing myself with not just one problem of the future, but like ten problems of the future. This was clearly a multidecade research agenda. And I was one of the first economists in the world to see it." It was an epiphany that launched her thinking in an entirely new research direction—all because she was willing to embrace uncertainty.

For doctoral students, navigating the academic landscape can feel akin to walking a tightrope. The journey is fraught with personal sacrifices, from leaving loved ones behind to grappling with the financial burdens of student loans. The pressure mounts as you race against time, eager to trade the title of student for a paycheck. In such high-stakes situations, the thought of taking risks can be daunting, akin to betting all your chips on a single roll of the dice.

Yet embracing uncertainty doesn't necessitate a blind leap into the abyss. It's about taking a step back and assessing your arsenal—your skills, knowledge, and the network of people ready to support you. It's about making informed decisions that strike a balance between risk and reward. Think of it as playing chess, not roulette; each move is calculated, with a clear understanding of the potential outcomes.

Having a backup plan and seeking guidance from mentors can provide a safety net, allowing you to embrace risk with a bit more confidence. It's not about eradicating uncertainty altogether—that's an impossible feat. Instead, it's about finding a way to navigate the unpredictable waters in a manner that aligns with your personal aspirations and circumstances.

Opportunities Arise from Your Actions

One hallmark of an entrepreneur is their ability to transform situations into opportunities. While others might see obstacles, entrepreneurs perceive potential. Their alertness, prior knowledge, and knack for pattern recognition enable them to identify opportunities. We each have the capability to adjust our mindset to recognize and seize opportunities and take action. As Brian Bergman, a professor of entrepreneurship at Tulane puts it, you need to be listening—you need to have your antennae up. "When you go into situations, are you looking to add or create value? When you are in a networking situation, it doesn't help to think 'how can I get something out of this?' Instead, think 'how can I give something to this environment?'"

This concept of creating opportunities can be applied by leveraging knowledge from past experiences to address present circumstances, which often involves making connections between seemingly unrelated elements. Lucy Partman, a lecturer at Princeton University, frames being an entrepreneurial scholar as having "an awareness of different audiences. You are looking for opportunities in the present, but also recognizing what came before and what might be possible after."

Partman epitomizes the ability to make connections across different times and spaces. During her graduate studies, Partman specialized in American art and visual culture, with a focus on the intersections of visual culture, science, philosophy, education, and performance. When I spoke with Partman about her diverse interests, she told me, "I'm always looking for new environments to test out, explore, and see what might be possible. During undergrad, I was majoring in art history and biology, I was doing visual arts, I was working in art conservation and in biology labs. I have found that new insights come from being in a lot of different spaces and then figuring out how they connect and can come together."

For Partman, connecting disparate ideas also means pursuing activities unrelated to her dissertation. As a doctoral student, Partman was involved in multiple organizations and initiatives. "Being open and experimenting with different types of projects is an attitude and approach that is different from focusing on the dissertation at the exclusion of everything else. The latter can actually limit your perspective on your research. By becoming involved in different facets of the university, you get to see how knowledge is produced and operates in the much larger ecosystem." By immersing herself in spaces outside of her department, Partman was able to create opportunities for herself. As a postgraduate research associate, she created and now leads a new experimental transdisciplinary course called "Looking Lab: Experiments in Visual Thinking & Thinking about Visuals," where students apply visual thinking practices from a range of real-world fields to design new tools to help people engage with each other.

Graduate school is traditionally seen as a path to becoming an expert in your field, focusing on mastering existing literature and conducting independent research. However, adopting an entrepreneurial mindset reframes this journey as an investment in your broader human capital—developing practical skills and experiences that are valuable both within and beyond academia. This approach emphasizes the importance of not only your intellectual ideas and theoretical knowledge but also your personal competencies. Embracing the role of an entrepreneurial scholar means proactively shaping your future and creating opportunities. Graduate school is an incredible opportunity to improve such skills (generally for free) and doing so increases an academic's value in any job market. In graduate school, I even took several storytelling and improv classes in the communications department— mostly with undergraduates! Turns out, learning to think on your feet and entertain a crowd isn't just for aspiring comedians; it's a secret weapon for academics too. The more skills that scholars develop at any point in their career, the less stuck and constrained they will feel when they start considering their next career move.

What does that entail? First, *begin by exploring educational opportunities outside your field and read beyond your discipline.* Even with a specific research focus entering graduate school, remain open to exploring various avenues and directions. This approach can lead to unexpected connections and insights. Christian Smith, a sociologist at Notre Dame, emphasizes the importance of "cross-pollination" in academic work. He notes, "Many intellectual advances come when people bring ideas or frameworks from some other sphere into their field. Some stimulating ideas in sociology of religion came from totally different spheres like economics. It doesn't mean I agree with it, but it's at least stimulating to think about. Talking to people who have thoughts and ideas and perspectives that are very different is crucial in all this. Otherwise, we just become intellectually shrunken."

Dalton Conley's academic journey exemplifies this concept. Initially earning a PhD in sociology, Conley later pursued a second doctorate in biology, underscoring his commitment to lifelong learning and interdisciplinary exploration. He advises, "Your education is not over. If you're going to be a lifetime scholar, you should keep taking classes because the field evolves." Conley views a scholar as an "import-export dealer of ideas," bringing together concepts, knowledge, and methods from various domains. This approach led him to integrate ideas from economics into his sociological research, particularly in his work at the National Center for Children in Poverty. While presenting data at the Robert Wood Johnson Foundation's annual conference, Conley's findings on the relationship between a child's birth weight and future socioeconomic status caught the attention of an economist. This interaction spurred Conley to delve into econometrics, ultimately enriching his sociological research and leading to new discoveries.

Second, *pursue projects outside of your dissertation.* Although grad students often feel like they should work exclusively on their dissertation, it might help to limit your workday and pursue other projects or endeavors. Think of yourself as a "proactive, self-directed, omnivorous learner who follows your interests no matter where they might lead," says Paula Chambers, a film director who became an English professor, and then created a LISTSERV for people looking for jobs outside academia. "The ability to do many things competently, to move freely in all directions, to learn anything under the sun on an as-needed basis, is a superpower."[9] Dalton Conley worked several side jobs while pursuing his PhD, including as a contract journalist. This experience taught him how to discipline himself when it comes to writing and how to write quickly and efficiently. Now, when graduate students tell him they are stuck in their writing, he has them sit in his office while he gives them a finite period of time (usually two hours) to write one section of an article.

Tamara Gilkes Borr also pursued side jobs that weren't directly related to her research, which benefited her when she was considering her career options: "Throughout my PhD, I was doing the things I wasn't 'supposed to do.' Instead of spending my whole summer doing my own research, I worked for the College Board. I spent Fridays working for Kamala Harris when she was attorney general, and I did work for the prison university project. It's important for grad students to know that they should keep doors open." Borr believes that some people thought she was wasting her time by doing things that took her away from her research agenda. But in reality, she spent a lot of time doing things that allowed her to transition out of academia. "Rather than seeing that time away from my research as a waste, it was an opportunity to open other doors . . . you never know when opportunities will arise." Borr landed a job at *The Economist* because she started freelancing in her sixth year of graduate school and writing for places like *The Atlantic*.

Managing Risk by Failing Forward

In April 2023, while writing this book, my kids and I were listening to NPR's coverage of the SpaceX launch on our way to school. The specifics of the SpaceX launch were complicated, but the central message was clear: SpaceX seemed excited about the prospect of failure. "Why are the people happy that the rocket might explode?" one of my kids asked. I thought this was a great question. It turns out that SpaceX's philosophy centers on failure. They use failure as a basis for their designs. They push their hardware to its maximum capacity until it breaks or explodes, and then they analyze what went wrong and learn from it.[10] Fail fast, but learn faster, they say. About four minutes into its flight the rocket did in fact explode. Rather than seeing this as a failure, SpaceX saw this as a learning experience that would help in the development of future spacecraft: "Success comes from what we learn," they tweeted.

Many great inventions were preceded by failures. Thomas Edison experienced more than a thousand failures before successfully inventing the incandescent light bulb. Other failures by Edison that ultimately led to successful outcomes included an electric pen, an automatic vote recorder, a tinfoil phonograph, and even a talking doll. Rather than seeing his failures as setbacks, he saw them as opportunities to learn and improve his design: "I have not failed 10,000 times—I've successfully found 10,000 ways that will not work," he said.[11]

Failure is scary. It is especially scary if you haven't experienced much of it before and don't feel equipped to handle it well. People who are used to being excellent—who have won lots of academic prizes—are especially terrified of experiencing failure. If someone ends up in a PhD program, chances are high that when it comes to academics, they were often quite successful. The prospect of failure for these individuals can feel terrifying, because for them the cost of falling short, even temporarily, becomes not merely practical but existential. The result is a damaging aversion to risk.[12]

Dealing with uncertainty often creates a sense of panic that leads people to adopt a more cautious and risk-averse mindset, opting for certainty over chance. However, this poses a challenge for creativity, which involves taking exploratory risks in order to push beyond the boundaries of what is currently known and to generate new and innovative ideas. As careers consultant Sophia Donaldson wrote in a blog advocating for academics to think like entrepreneurs, "Risk tolerance isn't a typical part of personalities drawn to academic research."[13] She points out that although academics are great at locating weaknesses in ideas, when it comes to experimenting with new ideas, they tend to be pretty conservative by avoiding things that feel risky. This creates a contradiction, where the pursuit of the unknown is at odds with the desire for certainty.

Constantina Katsari, a tech entrepreneur who received her PhD in history, puts the tension between certainty and risk like this: "Academic thinking is all about perfectionism. It's about doing things so perfectly that you never fail. But as an entrepreneur, I have learned that I need to fail and fail fast and fail often so that I learn more. Of course, I don't consider this a failure. I consider this extreme learning. And the more I fail, the more I learn. If you go and tell that to academics, they will look at you like you came from another planet because you're not supposed to fail your publications. I know entrepreneurs that go bankrupt and then still raise another round of funding and go ahead and do something else very successful."

Part of the aversion to risk and failure among scholars might reflect the fact that people who have been constantly praised for their intelligence often develop a fixed mindset rather than a growth mindset. As psychologist Carol Dweck posits, in the fixed mindset, people perceive their talents and abilities as set traits. They believe that brains and talent are enough for success and their goal is to look smart. They think they are either good at something or they are not. When people with a fixed mindset are frustrated, they give up. When they fail, they assume that means they are not smart. They believe that their output is largely determined by ability. In the growth mindset, people believe their abilities can be developed though dedication, effort, and hard work. They think brains and talent are not the key to lifelong success but merely a starting point. They believe they can learn anything they want to. When they are frustrated, they persevere. People with a growth mindset want to challenge themselves, and when they fail, they realize that it is an opportunity for learning. They believe that their output is largely determined by their attitude and effort.[14] For Elaine Ecklund, professor of sociology at Rice University, a growth mindset is central to her scholarship and career. "I love being challenged. I like personal growth, and I hope I never stop growing. I feel fortunate to have the kind of job where I can always encounter new things."

People might think that a growth mindset means that entrepreneurs are unfazed by failure, but this isn't true. What is different is that they both expect failure (whereas most academics don't) and they have a different way of dealing with failure. Eric Ries, author of *The Lean Startup*, describes his feelings after his first start-up failed:

> If you've never experienced a failure like this, it is hard to describe the feeling. It's as if the world were falling from under you. You realize you've been duped. The stories in the magazines are lies: hard work and perseverance doesn't lead to success. Even worse, the many, many, many promises that you've made to employees, friends, and family are not going to come true. Everyone who thought you were foolish for stepping out on your own will be proven right ... it wasn't supposed to turn out this way ... There is a myth-making industry hard at work to sell us that story, but I have come to believe that the story is false.[15]

Ries offers this corrective: "The grim reality is that most start-ups fail. Most new products are not successful. And most new ventures do not live up their potential." This might seem like a very bleak outlook, but what distinguishes entrepreneurs is the mindset with which they face this reality. It radically changes their relationship with failure and how they deal with it.

Entrepreneurs have a "fail forward" mentality, which is essentially learning by doing. When you fail forward, you use it as a learning experience to advance things. You do it quickly, and you bounce back up on your feet almost before you hit the ground—nothing more and nothing less. Contrary to the perception of being high-risk takers, entrepreneurs actually engage in calculated risks. They follow an act-learn-build cycle, where small actions lead to learning, which then informs the next set of actions.[16]

In the entrepreneurial world, there are individuals who always look for the silver lining, who see potential in every situation and move forward with optimism. On the other hand, there are those who "fail backward," spending excessive time dwelling on their failures, assigning blame, or wallowing in self-pity. These attitudes can hinder progress and growth.[17]

The same principles apply to successful entrepreneurs and academics. Because entrepreneurship takes place in a difficult and unpredictable environment, persistence helps overcome setbacks and correct one's mistakes. Companies often release products before they are perfect, and they improve them in future iterations once they have customer feedback. Scholars will inevitably face a tremendous amount of rejection, but the feedback from grant and journal article reviewers can help them refine their ideas. Of course, it's perfectly fine to give yourself a 24-hour "anger pass" when that article rejection comes in. Despite how it feels, Reviewer #2 doesn't actually hate you—they're just really passionate about table formatting!

When you see the CV of your professors and scholars you admire, it's easy to see a success story. But for younger scholars, rejections from journals, conferences, and grants may be especially devastating and demotivating because they do not realize how common it is. I once attended a session with three professors, including my advisor, who shared their rejection CVs. They revealed their unpublished papers, unfunded grant proposals, and job rejections. This transparency about their setbacks and perseverance was reassuring, reminding me that such experiences are part of the academic journey.

After a paper of mine—which I thought was brilliant at the time—was rejected in graduate school, I took great solace in the story of Mark Granovetter, a renowned sociologist, whose paper "The Strength of Weak Ties" was initially rejected by the *American Sociological Review*. The paper was published (four years later!) with a different framing in the *American Journal of Sociology*.[18] It has been cited over 72,000 times. Yes, even groundbreaking research can be met with skepticism and resistance at first.

In sum, failure is a mentor to be embraced. Entrepreneurs who push through doubts and keep pushing forward know this well. Their setbacks are stepping stones to learning and creating something new. But let's be real: not every entrepreneur hits the jackpot. If you've got a dud of an idea, sticking with it through thick and thin might not be the smartest move. The key is knowing when to switch gears and adopt a "fail fast, fail often" mindset, treating each misstep as a chance to learn something. As Rosa Arriaga, a graduate advisor and human computer interaction researcher at Georgia Tech puts it, "Don't think of it as failure. Think of it as feedback." And that rejected paper that I thought was brilliant? I never published it. The reviewers were right—it was very flawed. But I did use the feedback to improve the ideas in the article and used those ideas to write my first book.

So if you ever feel down about a rejection, just remember, you're in good company. Even the most cited papers had their humble, and sometimes bumpy, beginnings. And who knows, maybe one day, your rejected paper will be the stuff of academic legend.

Embracing Options outside Academia

It's certainly true that for many people in the past, a PhD meant you could secure an academic position, but since this is no longer realistic for most graduate students, they need to change their expectations. Academics need to recalibrate because the odds of getting an academic job are very low, and much of it is based on luck. If the only viable plan someone has is to get a tenure-track job, it is likely that they will be much less able to manage the letdown of potentially not getting one, causing them to end up feeling like a failure. However, the truth of the matter is just the opposite. Someone's ability to get a tenure-track position is not a reflection of their self-worth as a human being. As Gladys Ato, a clinical psychologist, former university president, and author of *The Good Goodbye: How to Navigate Change and Loss in Life, Love, and Work*, explains, "A big part of my process as an entrepreneur is when you take away the expectations that are imposed upon you by an institutional structure, when you take away the cultural norms of academia, you are left with this blank slate to create your own dreams and allow those dreams to flourish. That freedom can scare people. And it can actually hold us from diving right in."

It's precisely because the odds are stacked against scholars getting tenure that academics should instead think like entrepreneurs. Entrepreneurs already know that the odds of success are tiny, so they are not emotionally set back as much when their first design or business plan doesn't pan out. And an entrepreneurial mindset doesn't aim for a single goal, but rather prepares for a range of outcomes—including a life outside academia.

One key to overcoming that fear and reducing your reliance on an academic career is discovering that you have options. Taura Taylor, a professor at Morehouse College, entered graduate school in sociology years after working in mortgage lending and then as an auditor at the Department of Transportation in Georgia. She had also spent several years running her own natural hair business, something she continued to do to make ends meet in grad school. "I didn't feel that anxious energy about my career opportunities because I was already a business owner and I knew I had other options. Having this backup option also helped me feel courageous in graduate school. If you don't feel a sense of security, you don't want to rock the boat or ask provocative questions."

During my conversation with Teresa Mangum a professor at University of Iowa, she expressed a strong desire for graduate students to break free from the academic cocoon. She believes that by engaging directly with the world beyond their university walls, students can unlock the wider relevance and impact of their work and ideas. "Graduate students should actively network, seek internships, and explore diverse environments during their studies to truly understand their worth," she advised. Mangum emphasized that the skills honed in graduate school—such as analytical thinking, synthesizing complex information, crafting insightful questions, and listening intently—are invaluable in various professional settings. She urges students to recognize this and seek out opportunities beyond academia to apply these skills. These experiences can transform students' perspectives on their education, their potential career paths, and, most importantly, their confidence in their abilities.

In her essay "The Afternoon I Decided to Quit Academia,"[19] L. Maren Wood (PhD in history) reflects on feeling completely unprepared for any job outside of academia and her revelation that careers outside of academia look much different than what she suspected. In her mind, the only career path available to grad students went like this: grad student → postdoc → assistant professor → associate professor → full professor → professor emeritus → death. But outside of academia, people change their jobs every few years and often change their careers completely—some even several times. After leaving academia, Wood became an entrepreneur, which was not the result of years of planning, but rather "the product of a series of events, or opportunities." Wood went on to start the Center for Graduate Career Success, a mission-driven organization that partners with universities to prepare master's and doctoral students for career success. In 2019, Wood wrote an advice letter to herself in graduate school some fifteen years earlier.[20]

What you don't know at this moment is that this time you spend on your PhD, plus a few years post-graduation, will be your academic career. This dream that you have right now . . . won't happen for you . . . But the truth is, the reason why you feel so lost is that—academia is the only thing you've really known . . .

There is an enormous world full of opportunity. And you will thrive as an entrepreneur and CEO of a small start-up. You'll discover how challenging marketing and sales can be, about customer support and success. You'll coach and mentor and write. You'll lead a small team of passionate and committed people as you build something from scratch—a business . . .

You'll spend your time identifying problems, and then trying to solve them. You'll spend hours talking with new friends and mentors about how to solve these challenges . . . It turns out, what you're actually interested in is high level strategic thinking. You like solving problems. You're a creative thinker and problem solver. You love helping others and empowering people to be their best selves. These are things that matter to you. You'll want to spend time living in the cities you want, being with your partner, enjoying the challenges of running a business . . . You'll remain intellectually engaged and challenged. In fact, most nights when you head to bed, you'll be exhausted from all the intellectual challenges and problems you're working on. So, get the PhD. Love every minute of it. Just know that you are more than your degree. Your interests are not confined to your discipline.

Wood's story is an important lesson about an underappreciated fact among graduate students and early career scholars: there are wonderful and fulfilling jobs outside of the academy.

Graduate programs, especially at top universities and departments, still condition graduate students to believe that the only legitimate profession is the professoriate. Heather Frederick, a former university dean and host of *The Happy Doc Student* podcast, recalls that when she was applying to graduate school, saying you wanted to be a professor was the only appropriate answer: "I told my advisor that I wanted to do something in business. And my advisor was like, oh, no, no, no, you have to say, 'you want to teach and do research in a university setting.' That's how you get in—then once you have the degree, maybe you'll do something else."

In reality, chances are high that most graduate students will end up pursuing a job outside the academy. The chances are also high that their graduate program will not prepare them to do so. From an entrepreneurial perspective, the issue is not the lack of tenure-track positions (problematic as that is), but rather the fact that graduate students are unprepared for how to respond. As Lenny Cassuto puts it, "The simple and bounded search for an academic job causes too many graduate students to *un*learn how to look for other kinds of work."[21] That is why the onus is on graduate students to chart their own path. Each student is the CEO of their education.[22]

Graduate students can't control the outcome of the job market, but they can control their effort and attitude and therefore the meaning of their career journey. All that's needed is a willingness to "own their exit" and recenter their identity. According to Dan McAdams, a psychologist renowned for his theory of narrative identity,[23] you must change your story before you can change your life. By resetting your expectations,

you can better prepare for the unexpected twists that may—
and likely will—arise during your academic journey.

Why It Matters

McAdams is right—you can reset your expectations by exercising agency and rewriting your story—even if that means
writing a new story outside of academia. Sue Reinhold was a
Marshall Scholar who earned her PhD in social anthropology
at the University of Sussex. A young queer doctoral candidate
in anthropology, Sue was also a feminist and gay activist fight-
ing for marriage equality and gay rights. In 1991 at the height
of the AIDS crisis, the American Anthropological Association
held its annual meeting in San Francisco. Given its location in
one of the most important communities in the history of
American LGBT rights and activism, Reinhold expected to
see nuanced conversations featuring scholars doing ethnography and spotlighting people in the Bay Area who were doing
important work around AIDS and gay rights. But the AAA
merely organized a panel around AIDS with big-name people
in the field who knew absolutely nothing about the topic at
the local level. Reinhold was furious. This marked a turning
point for her, and she began the process of rewriting her story
by thinking about other ways she could continue doing research outside of academia.

A friend of hers said, "Sue, you love research. Why don't
you become a Wall Street analyst?" It wasn't something she
had ever thought about, so as she was wrapping up her PhD
she started doing informational interviews with people in the
industry and started studying for the chartered financial

analyst (CFA) exam. She was persistent in pursuing this opportunity, and at her *fiftieth* informational meeting, Reinhold
got her opportunity. She was introduced to an investment
manager who had recently launched his own firm. Eager to
impress, Sue presented a four-page analysis of a company she
believed was a hidden gem for stock investment: Koala Bear
Care, the unsung hero of diaper-changing tables in public rest-
rooms. Not exactly the poster child for excitement, but Sue's
analysis suggested potential high-profit margins. The firm's
owner, accustomed to hearing pitches for trendy stocks like
Intel, was taken aback but intrigued by Sue's unconventional
pick. "I'm gonna hire you," he declared. Reinhold rewrote her
story and has enjoyed a highly successful career in finance,
eventually starting her own investment firm and several other
entrepreneurial ventures. Who knew that the road to financial
success could be paved with diaper-changing tables?

Transitioning from being a successful student to becoming
a successful scholar while navigating uncertainty involves embracing the unpredictable nature of academia. Here are the
key points to keep in mind:

Embrace the unpredictability of academia: Thriving
in the academic world requires accepting its inherent
uncertainties. Success is not just about excelling in
structured environments but also about navigating the
unpredictable waters of scholarly work with agility and
resilience. Be open to unexpected opportunities that
come your way.

Seize opportunities through action: An entrepreneurial
mindset is characterized by a proactive approach to

creating opportunities. It's about leveraging who you are, what you know, and who you know to forge new paths and make a meaningful impact. Whenever possible, step out of your comfort zone, take courses and read outside your discipline, and engage in projects beyond your dissertation.

Fail forward with confidence: Managing risk in academia involves learning from failures and using them as stepping stones to success. Try to adopt a "fail forward" mentality so that you can view setbacks as valuable feedback that allow you to refine your ideas and strategies. This requires a growth mindset and the courage to take calculated risks.

Explore beyond academia: Recognizing that there are fulfilling career paths outside of academia is crucial for an entrepreneurial scholar. It's about valuing the skills and knowledge you've acquired during your graduate studies and understanding how they can be applied in various sectors. Embracing options outside academia opens up a world of possibilities for your career trajectory.

3

The Idea Business

NATE CLARK MOVED into a new home in Oakland right around Christmas 2017, a peak time for package thefts. After the house a few doors down was burglarized, Nate decided he wanted some kind of home security system. The house he was renting had an old ADT detector that wasn't hooked up and the landlord told Nate he was free to experiment with it. As a software guy interested in the advancement of "smart home" technology, Nate believed there must be some way to merge the sensors with the existing ecosystem. He spent several hours each night after his kids went to bed experimenting. Ultimately, he purchased a few cheap parts from Amazon and wrote a software package to make a security system out of the equipment he already had. He posted a readme document on GitHub with links to what you needed to recreate his system.

To Nate's surprise, many people started downloading his file and discussing it on community forums. He started to wonder if this signaled a real demand for such a product. Around the same time, Nate was starting to feel bored at his full-time job, so he launched a Kickstarter campaign to help finance his new venture. Nate did not have a clear idea of how his product would evolve, but he was driven to figure out a solution to a problem that others were facing.

Many ideas that have changed lives started when someone saw an opportunity to solve a problem and came up with a solution. Brian Chesky and Joe Gebbia started Airbnb in 2008 after they were unable to pay their monthly rent in San Francisco and decided to rent out air mattresses set up in their living room to attendees of a local design conference. Drew Houston founded Dropbox in 2007 after he kept forgetting his USB drive at home. These start-ups all began as ideas aimed at solving a problem.

It's my argument that scholars should also approach academia aiming to solve problems. But as Thomas Mullaney and Christopher Rea explain in their book *Where Research Begins*, most scholars wrong-headedly think about topics instead. Graduate students know the phenomenon well, as they are always asked about their research topic. But rarely are scholars asked about the problem they are trying to solve.

Scholars, like entrepreneurs, are in the "idea" business. But the idea business revolves around addressing problems or addressing challenges. As Gladys Ato observed, for academics "it all starts with an idea. And then what do we do with the idea? We expand it. That is exactly what entrepreneurialism is." While they're not out to make a profit, scholars spend years ideating, honing, marketing, and disseminating their ideas, hoping that they will inform or change how others think, feel, or behave. In academia, this is known as knowledge production.

This task of knowledge production might sound simple, but scholars struggle with it in part because of the way graduate school professionalizes people—often stripping away the passion that motivated them to attend graduate school in the first place. As Will Fenton, an expert in the digital humanities who earned his PhD in English, explains: "When you go through the grad training, they kind of break you down and then rebuild you. I think it's a struggle for a lot of early career scholars to reconnect with that imperative to actually produce knowledge rather than to situate themselves in existing knowledge." Nowadays it is too often the case that graduate students lose their sense of excitement that they came into graduate school with. "There should be joy in knowledge production," Fenton shared. "I think that gets lost in the scholarly rites of passage that everybody has to pass through. You just get so much negative feedback . . . It's really hard to think about yourself as somebody who's also contributing to the knowledge community rather than just benefiting from it."

The solution is not to turn graduate school into a meat grinder, where everything is oriented toward publication. That too would rob students of the joy of knowledge production—in no small part because what they would be producing would unlikely be genuinely original and likely demotivating. As Sophie von Stumm, a professor of education and psychology, and her colleagues have argued, "Students who are pressured to finish their theses as quickly as possible, to publish too many papers or to attend one conference after the other will lose their curiosity for research." Instead of a forced march to a predetermined finish line, "students should make sure that they are looking forward to learning something new in each of those activities, rather than merely completing them because the supervisor or the school expects it."[1]

Graduate students and emerging scholars aren't the only ones who struggle to think expansively about ideas. Even seasoned academics tend to be constrained in their thinking. "Most people in academia do not like change. They like the status quo," observed Ato. "What I love about the for-profit sector is the entrepreneurial spirit. The ability to move nimbly, but also the adaptability to change." That said, she was quick to add that even academics can change: "It's not a title on your office door that gives you that ability to expand."

What's the Problem

To break free of this mold and become an entrepreneurial scholar means being someone who generates ideas. Contributing to knowledge begins with the very difficult task of identifying a problem.[2] As Michael Weisbach, author of *The Economist's Craft*, explains, "Ultimately, the most critical ability for researchers is their aptitude for identifying intriguing problems and solving them through creative means."[3] Alison Miller, founder of The Dissertation Coach, agrees that there is a link between creativity and problem-solving: "Creativity is the tendency to be able to generate or recognize ideas, alternatives, possibilities that could be useful in solving problems." For her that's almost synonymous with being entrepreneurial. "Entrepreneurship is kind of an energy—it's a way of looking out at the world, seeing problems and wondering how they can be solved."

Mullaney and Rea suggest starting with "self-centered research," which means discovering what matters to you and framing it as a problem that can be investigated. You have to first uncover what matters to you and separate that from everything else (including what you think your dissertation advisor or the field wants). Is there a problem in the world you care about? What motivates and engages you? What is the impact you want to make relative to this problem?

Josh Ladon entered his part-time doctoral program at the Jewish Theological Seminary already thinking in terms of problems. He had spent several years working at different think tanks and educational institutions, and he had developed a set of concerns and questions in his field of Jewish education that he didn't know how to study or make sense of. Graduate school was a chance to figure out how to connect and investigate them—a means for solving the puzzle. "The PhD was a vehicle to think in new ways." He saw graduate school as an opportunity to "push on the conventions around a body of knowledge that everyone else accepts, and ask, 'Is that true? Is that how it works?'" For him the existing answers didn't "scratch my itch. There's something people haven't noticed before. I thought there is a different way of seeing it."

Kimberly Gramm also pursued her PhD to scratch an itch. Gramm, the chief innovation and entrepreneurship officer at Tulane University, started her career working as a corporate marketing strategist at UPS, then pivoted by taking a role building strategy for an entrepreneurship center at a university. Years later, Texas Tech recruited her to build an innovation district—a hub where institutions, companies, and organizations come together to foster innovation, collaboration, and economic growth. These districts typically include research institutions (such as universities), businesses (especially start-ups and high-tech firms), and support organizations (like incubators and accelerators). The goal is to create an environment that promotes innovation and entrepreneurship by facilitating the exchange of ideas, resources, and talent among its members. Gramm was charged with leading economic and industry engagement, increasing start-up development, and expanding commercialization programs for faculty and students. This was a lofty goal, so Gramm decided to tap into the expertise of her university's faculty. While meeting with an entrepreneurship professor, he encouraged Gramm to take his class. She decided to take him up on the offer and soon found herself surrounded by PhD students discussing topics like entrepreneurial cognition research and stakeholder theory.

As the only student with firsthand experience in the real-world contexts that her PhD peers discussed theoretically, Gramm found the scholarly literature lacking. It didn't provide her with insights into how university leaders could create the right conditions and allocate resources to help innovators and entrepreneurs effectively spread their ideas. At the time, Gramm was on a strategic planning committee for the university where each college and department had a representative. Gramm wondered how such a committee could set the course of an institution when everyone had different research agendas. Nothing in the scholarly literature helped her figure out how innovation ecosystems work. But when Gramm started asking these questions in class, her professor gave her an unexpected answer: go get your PhD and figure it out. Gramm was sold. For her dissertation, she interviewed leaders in universities of different sizes so that she could scratch her itch and better understand the innovation ecosystems within higher education.

Entrepreneurs who develop great products often have an "entrepreneurial alertness"—the ability to notice business opportunities without searching for them. Josh Ladon knew enough to know that the already existing answers were unsatisfactory. "There is a push and pull—you need to have the foundational knowledge so that you can say, 'I am not quite satisfied with it.'" Entrepreneurial scholars correspondingly are constantly thinking about gaps in the knowledge marketplace. Eddie R. Cole described how his research during graduate school at Indiana University emerged from his observations of how education was shaped by race. As a Black man, Cole was driven to pursue his research when he realized that the foundational readings in higher education history didn't reflect his community nor his personal experience. For example, a story that NPR aired about colleges seeking out rural students frustrated Cole because the story reflected a narrative of mainstream white institutions, while historically Black colleges and universities had been recruiting rural students for quite a long time (including Cole's own parents and grandparents). "My family's perspective on higher education history wasn't fully articulated. And the people who did touch on it had more of an outsider interpretation of things." Thinking about who he was and what he knew made it easy for Cole to identify gaps in the literature and come up with ideas.

Paige Harden, a psychology professor we met earlier, acknowledges that the transition from consuming knowledge "to thinking about what problems you find interesting (and what problems other people find interesting) is hard." It requires creativity, and too often academics don't think of themselves as creative. Susan Sidlauskas, associate professor and graduate director of the Department of Art History at Rutgers

University, admits that there is an enormous amount of background understanding that goes into creative thinking, and that coming up with problems doesn't happen on a timeline. "That deepening happens in fits and starts, and almost never on the schedule you imagined . . . A nearly unimaginable amount of tedium is part of every ambitious project."[4] But at the end of the day creativity lies within, and the problems that are truly worth solving are *your* ideas: "A genuinely original idea comes from deep within yourself and must be fortified by all the pertinent evidence that you have had the imagination, patience, and rigor of the mind to gather."

When Sarah Benor, a professor of contemporary Jewish studies and linguistics at Hebrew Union College sees a gap, she starts imagining how to solve the problem. For example, as an undergraduate Benor recognized that wherever Jews have lived around the world, they have spoken and written in language distinct from their non-Jewish neighbors—from Yiddish and Ladino to Judeo-Italian and Jewish Malayalam. Yet because of migrations and other historical events, many of these languages are on the verge of extinction. Benor thought it was imperative to document and raise awareness about these languages in the next decade—not only to record their last speakers but for the sake of Jewish children who would benefit from knowing about their multifaceted heritage. In 2020, Benor started the Jewish language project, convincing numerous organizations and scholars to document endangered languages. Over 1.3 million people have visited the program's website, and they have reached thousands of others through online events, videos, and educational social media posts.

Honing the Problem

How does a scholar hone their research problem? Being a scholar means conducting research that speaks to questions that are unsettled or at play. Ask yourself, what are the kinds of boundaries of the existing knowledge and how might I be able to expand the boundaries? There needs to be some tension and conflict—some knowing and some unknowing. How does your knowledge fit into the landscape of existing knowledge and where can you expand it? James McLurkin, an engineer who left his faculty position at UT Austin to pursue a job at Google, describes the process like this: "You need to figure out where the limits of the existing knowledge are in your particular area. And then you have to figure out how to ask the *next* question."

For Ken Bain, a former professor of history who became a scholar of teaching and learning and wrote the award-winning book *What the Best College Teachers Do*, entrepreneurial scholarship means connecting the ideas of others to your insights. "Part of the creative process is being able to recognize good ideas when I encounter them and to integrate them into my own. Creative life—or entrepreneurship—means recognizing your own uniqueness and other people's and going to school on their experiences and ideas." David Labaree, emeritus professor of higher education at Stanford, agrees; while you can't just repeat the ideas of others, creativity doesn't mean you can't use their idea: "You can't just be repeating what others have said or rehashing the familiar. You must find an angle that's fresh and intriguing for the reader . . . The key is that you're developing a novel approach to a familiar subject, using a [scholarly] scalpel to cut through the subject and producing a slice that shows it in a different light."

I took this advice when trying to come up with a research question for my dissertation. When reading a study by the Pew Research Center about the religious landscape of the US, I was surprised to learn that it was the most devout country among other rich nations. We know that race, social class, and gender influence children's attitudes toward and behaviors in school. Might religion influence educational outcomes in K-12 and in college in a similar way? After digging into the literature, I realized that not a single book had been written on this question. I had found my problem.

In locating their problem in an existing body of work, graduate students are often advised to narrow their focus early on, concentrating on just their little area of expertise and awaiting tenure to broaden their scope. Sociologist Christian Smith thinks this is exactly the wrong kind of approach an entrepreneurial scholar should take. "It's better to jump in and start swimming," he says. In his view graduate school is not a kiddie pool but a vast ocean that needs to be mastered and crossed. He's not alone in this opinion. As Weisbach notes in *The Economist's Craft*, the research interests of many early career scholars are so narrow in focus that there is little substance, and he sees this stemming from dissertations that take on a tiny problem and separate it from its larger context.[5] In David Labaree's view, "Many dissertation projects these days are so technical that they've lost their intellectual interest."

Labaree acknowledges the challenges faced by students who are taught to prioritize rigorous methodology in their research. He explains, "Part of the professionalism and the machinery of grad school is designed to make you rigorous. Rigorous first means have a methodology that is rock solid and staying close to your data." However, he argues that groundbreaking ideas often require stepping beyond this strict adherence to process and data. Labaree elaborates:

> The problem is that interesting ideas are generally two steps away from the data. There has to be some reading between the lines for you to be able to tell a story. The story isn't just going to emanate cleanly from the data. People feel nervous about taking the risk to make those connections. Yet some of the most interesting books I've read that make connections between ideas take those risks.

Labaree's perspective highlights the tension between the constraints of academic training and the creative leaps necessary for innovative research.

Strong technical skills are certainly important and valuable in scholarship, but when it comes to idea generation, nothing holds a candle to the question of thinking big. Simply "interrogating" the data won't produce entrepreneurial insights that will be valued by academia. There must be an interesting story to tell about why the problem even matters in a broader context. A gap in research is not a good enough reason to write a dissertation. Step back and ask: Why does that gap even exist?

Ken Bain illustrates his ideation process using a jigsaw puzzle metaphor: "I start writing and just throwing ideas on the page. And that leads me to do some more research and throw some more ideas on the page. I'm creating a lot of different pieces all at the same time." Initial attempts at putting them together often result in more material being generated. "While

I'm doing that, I may have another idea that says, 'No, this belongs over here.' So I create another piece." Then comes the hard work of assembling them. "I might jump over here and work on the one idea that will end up sixth, and then go back and forth."

It turns out that flexibility is essential to being entrepreneurial, as big ideas may require a change of direction. Yehuda Kurtzer, who turned down a tenure-track job offer to develop a think tank, encourages scholars to be open to pursuing lines of inquiry that they didn't plan for: "There are moments in the research process where scholars say, 'Wow, that's a really interesting finding, but it's totally not related to my thesis. So what I'm going to do is signal this would be an area of fertile area for further research, and then I will go back to my research project.' But it takes a very different kind of readiness or fortitude to say, 'I just found something that's really interesting and different. It wasn't what I set out to do, but I am going to refocus around that finding, even at the cost of the sunk effort that I've already put in on the original project.'"

I mentioned earlier how I came to find my research problem. What I didn't mention was that this problem was completely different than what I had proposed when I started graduate school. Initially, I was fascinated by the question of why children disengage from Sunday school after their bar or bat mitzvah. This curiosity led me to conduct a year-long ethnography. However, my research took a dramatic turn when I encountered the Pew report on America's religious landscape. Confronted with broader and more compelling questions, I approached my advisor with a proposal to shift my focus from Jewish education to the broader interplay between religion and education in America. This pivot not only expanded the scope of my inquiry but also enriched my understanding of American Jewish life.

Christian Smith advises students to pursue projects that are broad for an additional reason: "Err on the side of studying something big, something important, something that people know already, something where if you give them the one sentence, they know why it's valuable." Rather than filling a tiny gap by extending our knowledge a little bit, he thinks graduate students should try to choose stuff that matters in the world—something that people, even if they personally don't connect to it, will conceptually get why it is important.

Caring about the Problem

Motivation is a key step to doing the kind of research that is a precursor to generating influential ideas. An internal drive and search for answers generally motivates the best research. This is how entrepreneurs treat their ideas, projects, concepts, or products—they care so deeply about their problem that they are willing to go the extra mile and overcome all the negative feedback. If a scholar is not deeply interested in their research problem, it's not only that they will not be able to sustain the motivation to keep going—the challenge is getting others interested in your problem. As McGill sociologist Eran Shor puts it, "If you don't care about what you're doing, then it's very hard to convince others to care." For Elaine Ecklund, "There's a real goodness to knowing what you enjoy, especially in academic work. If we don't enjoy the work, it's very hard to put in long hours. Very few of us are able to do this just as a job."

Of course, often the problems you are truly interested in aren't clear when you start. Motivation is essential to getting to the bottom of them. David Zvi Kalman started his PhD with an interest in Islam. He was learning Arabic and spending time in Cairo, but Kalman struggled to find the motivation to work on his research. One day his wife pointed out that he was interested in something he hadn't recognized: clocks. She told him that he should make clocks the focus of his academic work. Kalman started to wonder how Jews responded to the development of timekeeping technology, which turned out to be the most promising way of carrying his interest forward into a substantial academic project. After his dissertation, he realized that he had important insights to contribute to other debates about technology and religion—everything from why pork made out of "impossible meat" shouldn't be kosher to why French Jewish philosopher Emmanuel Levinas would have argued against the morality of facial recognition technology.

If a graduate student is writing a dissertation solely to appease their committee or secure a future academic position, they risk falling out of love with their research and losing the drive to continue. Melissa Dalgleish, who received her PhD in Canadian literature, captured this feeling as she reflected on how her motivation changed once she realized that there were amazing jobs outside of academia and that she had the skills for them. This insight freed her to write a dissertation that *she* cared about rather than one that (to her thinking) was more geared toward a tenure-track position: "I spent a lot of time figuring out why I was writing this book, a book that few would read, if not to get a job. It was very slow going until I started writing a book that I had long wanted to, and one that had (and has) intrinsic merit beyond its value on the academic job market."[6] The trajectory of your dissertation can set the course for years of research, so it's paramount to choose a topic that genuinely captivates and matters to you.

Ken Bain was a political historian who had written books on US foreign policy. But as an educator, he became curious about what it means for college professors to teach and what it looks like for students to learn. To venture away from US foreign policy and write books about how people learn, what it means to learn, and how to foster learning was a big risk. Many people initially advised him against doing so, saying it wasn't appealing or valuable, but Bain felt it was important: "My response was, 'I'm gonna make it respectable.'" Bain admits it was an arrogant attitude on his part, but that feeling is what motivated him. His first book, *What the Best College Teachers Do*, ended up being a big hit and won several awards.

It is quite possible that the ideas you are motivated to study are not the ones your discipline will encourage or reward. Seth Stephens-Davidowitz came into the economics program at Harvard excited to use clever methods to explore big questions like, "How did racism influence how people voted for Obama?" However, his advisors quickly dismissed his ideas: "That's so *Freakonomics*," they said disparagingly, and advised him to pursue issues like inflation and interest rates that were seen as "real economics." There was just one problem: Davidowitz wasn't interested in those issues. He decided to pursue the questions he felt motivated by, though he recognized that it precluded him from being able to land an academic position. He pivoted by taking a job at Google, but continued to write and research the topics he loved. In 2017, he published *Everybody Lies*, which ended up being a *New York Times* bestseller.[7]

Computer scientist Matt Welsh took an unconventional approach to his work in wireless sensing technology because he thought his research could help seismologists and geophysicists with a problem they had: tracking the three-dimensional activity of a volcano. He began putting sensors on volcanoes to build a 3D spatial model of what volcanoes are doing. Welsh approached the problem with a classic entrepreneurial mindset:

> I realized that this was an interesting problem area to work on and we were gonna learn a lot by going out in the field and working with these people, learning as much as possible about someone else's area and getting out of our comfort zone. We might find that what we learned is not terribly relevant to our field or we might find that we have ideas of how to help them. But let's go learn about everything that they do, and embed ourselves with them for a while and try to collaborate and see what comes of it.

It was rare for computer scientists to do this kind of applied fieldwork, and Welsh received a lot of pushback about trekking into the jungle when he could be doing experiments in his lab. But he was willing to take the risk and invoke the puzzled stares of colleagues because his foremost concern was that his research had real-world relevance: "It starts with the realization that seismologists and geophysicists had problems, and that if [computer scientists] just directed our attention and our energy to their problems, we could build a solution that allows them to do better science." Welsh also had an entrepreneurial attitude that put him in control: "My view was that if Harvard didn't give me tenure for having done the thing that I was passionate about, then either I didn't belong in academia, or I didn't belong at Harvard." Welsh did get tenure, but his pursuit of real-world problems inspired him to start his own business instead.

Stories like these show that academics will likely be happier if they stay true to themselves, a belief encapsulated in the advice that *Freakonomics* author Steve Levitt shares with grad students: "You should do the research you love, that's fun for you. And if it turns out that the economics profession loves it too, that's fantastic. Then you'll have an amazing academic career. And if it turns out the economics profession doesn't share your taste in research questions or approaches, that's okay too. It just tells you that you should be doing something different." For Levitt, the worst outcome is when people pursue ideas they don't care about and then get a job that doesn't interest them. "You just can't succeed in a profession that you're bored by."[8] Narketta Sparkman-Key summed it up well: "You will have advisors say, 'Don't research that—that won't get you tenure—research this instead.' But what's the point of getting tenure if don't enjoy doing your work?"

Personalizing the Problem

Murad Sabzali didn't start his career trying to be an entrepreneur. As an undergraduate at Northern Illinois University, Sabzali studied finance, biology, and marketing. After college, Sabzali worked for a chemicals and pharmaceutical company, where he helped develop and market new products. After a few years, Sabzali noticed that there weren't many ways for life science companies to market new scientific advances to researchers and clinicians. Doctors couldn't learn about (or even participate in the development of) products and services that could help them identify diseases early and increase the chance of successful treatment—the various genomic and medical diagnostic devices that could help their patients improve their quality of life. The solution, as Sabzali saw it, was a marketing and communications firm that had enough technological and scientific knowledge to help companies reach clinicians. Since companies like this didn't exist, he wondered if he should start one.

Pursuing this new venture meant leaving his secure position to pursue something much more risky but potentially much more interesting: "There was a fork in the road. I can stay in a very secure position, or I can go out and work with really interesting new technology, helping researchers and clinicians take their innovations to the next level." But Sabzali wasn't just interested in solving a problem in the market—he saw this as a way to contribute to wellness and health by helping companies with innovative technologies reach real patients. His company, CGLife, is now in its twentieth year and thriving.

Ineffective businesses often copy existing products or services without any innovative changes to these ideas, while self-starting entrepreneurs are able to differentiate their solutions from other businesses and create what's known as a comparative (or competitive) advantage. Howard Gardner saw his evolution as a scholar in these terms:

It was becoming clear to me that many people could design and carry out empirical psychological studies as well as I could, and there were many more young researchers who were technologically or technically far more skilled than I could ever hope to become . . . My competitive advantage lay elsewhere. I was curious; I could read rapidly and widely; I enjoyed synthesizing and resynthesizing. I could also write quickly and clearly; and I could address various audiences, including the intelligent general reader. And so, while continuing for decades to contribute modestly to the peer-reviewed empirical literature, and training my students in that science and art, I became more of a writer, and strove (with limited but not negligible success) to be a public intellectual.

Applying this notion to academia, scholars should consider what research ventures are novel rather than replicas of someone else's work. "If your project was conceptualized by somebody else, you're slotting yourself into being a worker in someone else's machine," says David Labaree. "You really have to push back from that and start creating space for yourself." But adopting an entrepreneurial approach to scholarship demands thinking about problems in not just a new light, but in your light.

Identifying problems that are yours often starts with thinking about who you are and what you know—and how that differs from what other people know. As a first step, it helps to own your expertise and not feel apologetic about it. In the film *CODA*, the central character, who is the child of deaf parents, tries out for the school choir. The music teacher says to her:

"There *are plenty* of *pretty voices with nothing to say. Do you have something* to *say*?" Entrepreneurial scholars ask themselves the same question: Do *I* have something important to say?

For Elaine Ecklund, answering that question is rooted in merging one's research problem with knowledge of oneself. "PhD students have to know who they are, and really center what they think is important in the world and why they're doing the PhD." But there are obstacles that can prevent scholars from owning their ideas. For example, embracing the idea that what you have to say matters tends to be harder for people like women and BIPOC scholars, who have been traditionally marginalized. Women in particular have been conditioned to not assert their expertise. "We're so encouraged to think that following rules and being cooperative is the path to success early on," observed Teresa Mangum. "But then once you move into spaces like graduate school and all kinds of careers, it's quite the opposite. It's the people who do take chances, who are very open to new ideas, who say 'I'm willing to experiment and fail and experiment again,' that then go beyond the very predictable kind of career to more exciting fulfilling careers."

That is why it is so important for underrepresented individuals and minorities to bring their positionality to the forefront of the spaces they are in. "If you come from a marginalized community and bring your perspective and expertise to the conversation, you've expanded the conversation for everyone there," explains Taura Taylor, a sociology professor at Morehouse. She recommends low-income individuals and women own their expertise from where they stand to counter how they are rarely seen as epistemic authorities. "I think of myself not so much as having intersecting identities but intersecting statuses. On the one hand, there is this disadvantage of being a Black woman, but there is so much privilege that I also have. I'm educated. I'm a US citizen. And I can create social change [by] bringing to light these narratives and experiences of other marginalized people."

Taylor's own research, which examines Black women and families, is not something others might see as important or relevant. But one man's neglect is another woman's opportunity, giving her the freedom to approach her scholarship from an entrepreneurial angle and break free of one-directional models of researching her questions, creating (in her words) "a unique collaboration between scholars and the community rather than just a bookshelf conversation between scholars."

Entrepreneurs regularly ask themselves what differentiates them from other competitors. Academics don't quite use this language, but the idea is the same. As Labaree suggests, graduate school may initially train scholars to conform to established norms and sound like their peers, but the true goal is to distinguish oneself within the field. It's essential to identify your unique contribution: What is your niche? What will you be recognized for? What will secure your tenure?

Dalton Conley provides a strategy for achieving this distinctiveness: cultivating multiple research streams. By developing two or three different lines of inquiry and articulating the future directions of your work, you demonstrate more than just adherence to your advisor's guidance. You show that you are an independent thinker with a broad and innovative research agenda. This approach not only sets you apart within your discipline but also positions you as a forward-thinking scholar capable of shaping the future of your field.

In essence, the challenge for academics is to navigate the fine line between fitting into the scholarly community and standing out with original contributions. This balance is crucial for career advancement and for making a lasting impact in your area of expertise.

It is likely that where you have a comparative advantage is in virtue of having some unique knowledge that enables you to pursue a research agenda. You need to understand the value of your own contributions. Do you bring technical skills? A unique dataset you created? Institutional knowledge or a creative approach? Try to use this comparative advantage to develop a reputation for being the best at addressing certain kinds of questions. For Narketta Sparkman-Key, this was access to data from HeadStart because she had been there for ten years previously, which would allow her to examine her unique problem—looking at parenting practices using instruments that hadn't been normed yet for diverse populations like refugees.

Why It Matters

Scholars need to see themselves as capable of generating insights that can change how other people think. They should think of themselves as an academic "hunter"—someone who will search for the truth wherever clues can be found while also remaining open to opportunities that may arise in their area of interest that they didn't plan for.

One question that has been of perennial interest to scholars across fields like economics, criminology, and sociology is whether drivers who are racial minorities are more likely to get speeding tickets than white drivers who drive exactly the same. To date, there hasn't been the right data to examine this question. You might have data on the number of speeding tickets given to white drivers and minority drivers, but that's not enough information to determine whether there's discrimination because there are all sorts of variables that impact the number of tickets handed out. Minority drivers might speed more than white drivers, or they might drive in neighborhoods where there's a greater police presence. You would need to have the right data to rule out these alternative explanations.

To answer this question, John List, whose baseball card convention experiments we learned about in the Introduction, realized that he needed to think entrepreneurially—to go outside of academia into the corporate world. List was in a comfortable position at University of Chicago when he decided to make a significant shift and become the chief economist at Uber and then Lyft. Working at these organizations gave List a "new sandbox" of data to use in order to gain insight into questions that were previously very hard to answer. The vast amounts of data that organizations like these collect also allowed him and his colleagues to answer questions that everyone was asking but no one could answer.[9]

Using data from Lyft, List and his coauthors were able to determine when and where the drivers were driving, their speed, and in most cases their race. They were then able to cross-reference the Lyft data with a dataset from Florida that listed the names and the times and the locations of every speeding ticket that was handed out. By comparing these two datasets, they could see exactly how often in a given neighborhood minority drivers and white drivers were speeding and how often they got tickets. It turns out that there is substantial bias on the part of the police: even when a minority driver and a white driver are driving exactly the same, the minority driver is about 25 percent more likely to be given a speeding ticket. Racism matters—especially when you can prove it.

When it comes to working in the idea business, remember that you are contributing to a whole world of ideas. Here are the key points to keep in mind:

Identify problems worth solving: Just like entrepreneurs who start with a problem to solve, scholars should focus on identifying meaningful problems that need addressing. This is the first step in the journey of creating impactful ideas.

Hone your problem: Once you've identified a problem, refine it. Explore its boundaries, understand its nuances, and think creatively about how you can contribute to solving it. This process of honing is essential for developing a focused and impactful research agenda.

Care about your problem: Passion is what drives persistence. Ensure that the problem you're working on is something you genuinely care about. This intrinsic motivation will help you navigate the challenges of research and inspire others to engage with your work.

Personalize your problem: Make your research uniquely yours by bringing your personal experiences, knowledge, and perspective to it. This personalization will not only make your work stand out but also ensure that you remain invested and motivated throughout your academic journey.

4

Leveraging Resources

IN APRIL 2019, José Riera, at the age of fifty, set his sights on Pullman, Washington, with a vision to embark on a PhD journey in language, literacy, and technology at Washington State University's (WSU) College of Education that fall. Riera's mission was clear: to champion the educational needs of those underserved by the system, particularly individuals with disabilities. He believed that a doctorate in education would equip him with the knowledge to harness technology for enhancing academic and professional opportunities for people with disabilities. However, Riera faced a daunting challenge: as an out of state student, the program's annual cost was around $54,000, and it offered no financial support. A traumatic brain injury years earlier and several years of hospital rehabilitation meant that he had used all his savings on medical care and health insurance. Riera needed to find a way to pursue his academic and professional aspirations without plunging into significant debt.

While Riera did not have money, he thought about what resources he did have. Riera had an MBA and his first career had been in the business sector, mostly working in finance and management roles at large companies and also starting his own entrepreneurial venture (which did not survive the 2008 recession). He was hopeful that by talking to a lot of staff and faculty on campus, he could find opportunities to offset his costs by leveraging his skills.

Riera also knew the value of relationship building: his support network, including close friends from Wharton, had helped get his life back on track after his accident. He didn't know anyone at WSU yet, but that would soon change. Having arrived on campus three months before the start of the semester, Riera started knocking on doors and developing relationships with people on campus, letting them know he was looking for assistantship opportunities and telling them about his skills. He knew he would have to be proactive about sharing his interests and telling people about his experiences, not just within the College of Education but in other departments as well. One faculty member whom he approached supervised all the language instruction labs on campus, and she was impressed with Riera's management experience and the fact that he spoke other languages. She invited him to become the assistant director at the Language Learning Resource Center and she successfully procured a budget allocation to cover his tuition and pay him an additional stipend.

In April 2020, as Riera was in the second semester of his PhD, his lab position was terminated when the campus shut down for the pandemic. Riera again turned to his network, quickly reaching out to people across the campus community. Being proactive earlier and having his name out in the community proved successful. First, he found out about an opportunity to organize events for the WSU Emeritus Society—retired professors who come together to learn and socialize. Because of COVID-19, Riera started planning virtual events and teaching retired professors to use Zoom. Second, he was able to leverage a relationship he had developed with a College of Education professor to work on a summer research project after his scheduled summer fellowship got canceled because of COVID-19.

Riera's story illustrates how important it is to knock on different doors and not to be afraid if they say no: "It's not a rejection necessarily. It's just more of an issue of prioritization and saying, well, maybe it's not the door that you need, but at least you leave a good impression so that in the future, if something were to come up, they do call you . . . You also want to make sure that you craft a very good message so that when people meet you, they not only remember who you are, but they want to know what you're passionate about and how you're helping yourself and others."[1]

During the summer of 2021, a faculty member did just that—remembered Riera. An adjunct position to teach finance and entrepreneurship at the College of Business had just opened up, and that faculty member recalled that Riera had spent years in the corporate sector. He called Riera to see if he'd be interested in the position. Teaching turned out to be an ideal opportunity for Riera, allowing him to bridge his experience in business with his passion for education. He taught for two semesters, which helped him offset some of the costs of his PhD.

In a world that often celebrates the lone genius, solitary inventor, or isolated scholar, there's a hidden truth that often goes unnoticed: no one achieves greatness in a vacuum. This chapter is about uncovering that truth, about revealing the power of community as the secret engine behind the success of entrepreneurial scholars. It's a journey into the heart of academia, where the most valuable resource isn't found in the quiet corners of a library or the secluded spaces of a lab, but in the bustling intersections of human connection.

Imagine the academic landscape as a vast network, a web of relationships where each node is a person, each link a potential collaboration, a shared idea, or a mutual support system. In this network, the most successful scholars are those who understand that their strength lies not in their individual brilliance but in their ability to leverage the collective wisdom, experience, and resources of their community. This chapter invites you to navigate the academic world with a new perspective, where the currency of success is not just knowledge, but the connections that make knowledge come alive.

Scholarship as a Community Sport

Contrary to popular myth, entrepreneurship is not an individualistic endeavor. The rugged individualism you hear about people like Jobs, Gates, and Zuckerberg distorts the reality. These stories might imply that their successes were achieved alone, which is not the case. According to Rob Lalka, an entrepreneurship professor at Tulane University, "At its core, entrepreneurialism is about problem-solving, and that involves bringing different people and ideas together." Entrepreneurship is a collaborative endeavor where individuals rely on collective experiences and seek to learn from others who have faced similar challenges. It goes beyond working on projects together to involve actively seeking out others and exchanging information. Through networking, entrepreneurs can access external resources such as grants, emotional support, and expertise, while also engaging in mutual learning and information sharing.[2]

I want to suggest that scholarship, like entrepreneurship, is better viewed as a community sport. For scholars, relationships serve a very similar purpose. A diverse network gives you broader perspectives and enables you to trade information and skills with people who have different experiences and backgrounds. While this might go against the image we have of scholars sitting alone in windowless offices or library stacks toiling away in isolation—an image that might seem especially true for people in the humanities or social sciences who are not part of labs and are mostly working on independent projects in archives—it's time to update that image in light of the reality. After all, as Descartes might say if he were a modern scholar, "I think, therefore I collaborate."

Part of the challenge for scholars thinking this way is that the concept of relationship building feels inauthentic and instrumental, especially when it is described as "networking." As psychology professor Paige Harden says, "The biggest hurdle for academics is getting over the idea that networking is necessarily insincere and sleazy." Networking is not about developing inauthentic relationships that graduate students and early career scholars use only to ask for favors. It is not about developing relationships just to gain personal advantage. Networking is about developing trusting relationships so that two people can help each other do their work better.

Building relationships in academia goes beyond merely advancing individual career prospects. It's about sharing important ideas and contributing to the broader academic community. As sociologist Christian Smith explains, there are two distinct approaches to networking in academia. Some scholars engage in networking with a primarily egoistic, self-promoting focus, which is not the ideal approach. On the other hand, there's a more benevolent form of networking, where the goal is to promote ideas and research that are valuable to the world, contribute to the common good, and enhance humanity's well-being. This approach does require promoting oneself, stepping out of one's comfort zone, and being ready to engage in debates and face criticism. However, the motivation behind this is not just personal career advancement, but a desire to make a meaningful impact on society.

People who think outside the box often talk to people who play in different boxes in order to get new ideas. Entrepreneurs who want to discover new ideas will often talk to people from diverse personal and professional backgrounds and run their ideas by people who have a range of expertise in their substantive area. Scholars, like entrepreneurs, should build bridges into different areas of knowledge by interacting with people they don't usually interact with. This might mean attending sessions at conferences completely foreign (yet still interesting) to you, having coffee with scholars from across other disciplines in your university or nearby universities, or reading books outside your domain.

For education professor David Labaree, one of the most personally and professionally rewarding experiences of his career was coming together with a group of philosophers and historians of education who lived throughout Europe. They would organize small conferences in places like Estonia and Belgium centered around different topics and workshop each other's ideas and papers. "The personal and professional came together, and we became good friends. And it wasn't just a one-shot deal—we became part of a scholarly conversation that had a structure around it." Scholars tend to spend a lot of time in their heads, ruminating on ideas. For Labaree, this group enabled him to finally articulate those ideas and advance them: "Now there was a group of people who were sharing stuff I could draw upon and I wasn't just thinking about crazy stuff on my own. It stimulated my ideas, and through our conversations, I generated ideas for two new books. Networking is where opportunities come from."

People who have complementary skill sets are especially valuable to each other as collaborators. If someone enjoys spending countless hours data wrangling but finds the process of writing to be draining or overwhelming, the perfect collaborator is someone who finds crafting prose to be energizing but who hates statistical analysis. When compatible, collaborating often yields better ideas than either party can develop on their own. David Zvi Kalman intentionally seeks out collaborations with people who have skills that he doesn't: "I want to create stuff, but I recognize the limits of my own skills. I can't draw, but I'm interested in illustration. So if I want to produce things that require those skills, I need to bring in other people, and the ideas snowball. The creative energy and the way that ideas can be honed when you're passing them back and forth between two or three can't be replicated."

The interaction doesn't even have to be purely positive. The long-time partnership of psychologist Daniel Kahneman and mathematician Amos Tverksy, which laid the foundation for the field of behavioral economics and reshaped our understanding of human decision-making, started out with Tversky giving a guest lecture in Kahneman's class and Kahneman hating it. They ended up arguing about the issues and came up with experiments to resolve the questions they had about how individuals make decisions. They constantly challenged each other's ideas, pushing the boundaries of their research, and fueling their collective intellectual journey.[3]

But the benefits can also be more pragmatic as well. For example, collaborative work creates accountability: it is a lot easier to stay committed and accountable to a project when there's someone else attached to it. In my case, by thinking about the resources I could leverage in my network, I was able to solve a problem with my research: there was too much of it—over seven hundred transcripts averaging two hours per interview. Like an entrepreneur, I set about asking myself: What are some creative ways to find low-cost or free help to deal with all this data? It turns out that there are quite a few. First, I found out about a program at a local community college where students could participate in research at Stanford in exchange for course credit. Second, I created a summer internship for a high-school student in the area who had cold-emailed me asking about research opportunities and used a grant to hire two fellow doctoral students as research assistants. And then, as I described in Chapter 2, I figured out how to hire eighteen undergraduate research assistants through the federal work-study program.

Navigating academia can feel mysterious, especially the first time doing something. People in one's network can help with making progress by offering their own examples, especially when graduate students and early career scholars are trying to learn complex information. After I had defended my dissertation and was thinking about writing a book, I had no idea what my first step should be. I needed advice from someone who was in a similar career stage as I was and who had experience getting a book contract. At the time, I was collaborating on a paper with another early career scholar named Landon Schnabel, who had done something that I thought was impossible: he had gotten not one but two offers from top-tier presses for an advance contract on his book proposal about gender and religion. "Explain to me how this works," I said to him one day over lunch. Schnabel explained his process, including which presses he met with, how the conversations with different presses began, and how long each phase lasted. He also graciously shared his proposal. Learning about Schnabel's experience gave me a mental blueprint and bolstered my confidence that a book contract was even possible for someone out of graduate school. There is likely a Landon Schnabel in your academic sphere—a colleague who can demystify the process of embarking on something new. But remember, you need to be proactive in seeking them out and asking for their wisdom.

Where to Look for Community

The goal of entrepreneurial scholars is to build a support system of like-minded peers so they can engage in mutual learning and information sharing. But where do you find such people?

Much like how investors support entrepreneurs, offering more than just financial backing, mentors play a crucial role in the academic journey. Investors act as thought partners, engaging deeply with the ideas, contributing to decision-making, and connecting entrepreneurs to a broader network of experts and resources. Similarly, mentors provide graduate students and early career scholars with their experience, knowledge, and wisdom. They can offer critical guidance, expand their network, and provide the psychological encouragement needed to navigate the academic landscape.

But being entrepreneurial also means seeking out "strangers" who can help, as well. Kelli Marquardt, now an economist at the Federal Reserve, was an economics student at the University of Arizona when she learned about research showing that ADHD rates vary depending on where a kid's birthday falls and when the school cut-off is for entry into the next grade. Marquardt wasn't surrounded by people who knew about ADHD, so she started to think about what kind of data might help her answer her questions. Her advisor helped connect her to people in the medical center, and someone who was an MD in her economics department set her up with his friend who is a psychiatrist. Ultimately, she was able to study the physician decision to diagnose ADHD in children and young adolescents by getting de-identified electronic health records and then using Natural Language Processing to analyze the data.[4]

Another route to forging relationships is by targeting people at other institutions whom you can meet at conferences. This doesn't mean going to conferences to meet famous people. As Nneka Dennie, a professor of history at

Washington and Lee University, explains, "When it comes to networking with faculty, don't be a clout-chaser. To exclusively pursue influential scholars obscures the fact that all of us, ranging from contingent to tenured faculty, are experts in our fields. Rather than trailing the biggest name in the room (and being embarrassed when you have nothing to say), be intentional about speaking with scholars whose interests have actionable connections to yours. Capitalize on relationships where you can foresee collaborations on panels and articles."[5]

Often, the most productive and generative relationships that develop are with people who are in the same "problem collective"—people who think about similar issues but perhaps in different ways. I started emailing people whose papers I was reading and asking them to have coffee when our paths crossed at conferences. Almost all of them agreed to meet with me. It was during one of those coffee meetings that I got the idea from someone to turn my dissertation, which was a set of individual journal articles, into a book.

Sometimes, the best collaborators come from disciplines other than their own, which means anyone's problem collective ought to include people from multiple fields. Lucy Partman is always looking for new environments to test out, explore, and find connections between the different areas she is learning about, which include visual arts, art conservation, and biology: "I like being in a lot of different spaces, and then figuring out how they come together." Tricia Bruce offered this insightful observation: "When we surround ourselves with others who share our gifts, we don't necessarily see our insights as special or as bringing something new to the table.

But when we surround ourselves with other audiences, you're the only person in the room with your particular perspective and skillset."

And of course, it would be counterintuitive for entrepreneurially minded graduate students and early career scholars to limit their network to only individuals within academia. Entrepreneurial scholars have a broad conception of who they view as potential knowledge producers, and networking outside of academia challenges traditional academic hierarchies. As Dennie observes, "Collaborating with community partners and university staff members creates a more equitable environment by encouraging intellectual exchange beyond classrooms and conferences." But beyond simply addressing inequalities, she is at pains to make clear an important point, that "scholars . . . have things to learn from people who are not in academia."[6]

Making time for serendipity is also an option. Around 2007, Eran Shor, a sociology professor at McGill, and a friend of his at Stony Brook University, answered an ad from a computer scientist who said he had developed a tool that enabled him to scrape the web and take tons of information from newspapers (this was before big data was a thing). Shor was interested in newspaper coverage but didn't know how this tool could help him. For a year and half, Shor and his friend met with this guy to just exchange ideas until finally they stumbled upon common ground. It took six years from the time they started meeting to their first publication, but it ended up being a highly fruitful collaboration that yielded several studies, including an article in the leading sociology journal, the *American Sociological Review*.

Serendipity can take a variety of forms. Steven Zhou, a PhD student in industrial and organizational psychology at George Mason University, joined Lunch Club, a website where AI technology matches you with somebody else for a 45-minute conversation each week: "I don't know if it's going to be a valuable use of my time, and maybe I'll waste 45 minutes. But I'm willing to take that risk, because there are moments where it becomes an absolutely amazing use of my time, like when I develop a relationship with someone I can collaborate with. One of my conversations led to me presenting my work at the University of Amsterdam!"

Leaning into the entrepreneurial approach also leads to unforeseen opportunities. Tricia Bruce emphasizes that curiosity is what motivates her to strike up conversations with people: "When I am at a conference, I am genuinely curious to learn about people. I don't network for selfish reasons or because I want to climb my way up to something, but it unintentionally often leads to opportunities. Every project that I've ever had, every book I've ever published, all these things track back to relationships that I built." Relationship building has been crucial for Bruce, especially when she decided to leave her tenured position so that she could have more freedom to do the kinds of research and writing aimed at influencing public discourse. She still needed library access so she could read academic journal articles and approval from the Institutional Review Board, but usually you need to have an affiliation with an academic institution to access these resources. Bruce had spent many years cultivating relationships, which she leveraged to become an affiliate of two different universities.

My interactions with emeritus professors have taught me that they are an amazing but often untapped resource. These are professors with deep expertise and connections who usually have a lot of time on their hands, yearn for opportunities to engage in intellectual discourse, and find deep satisfaction in mentoring. In fact, my dissertation stemmed from a mentoring relationship I developed with an emeritus professor named Lee Shulman.

In my third year of graduate school, Lee and I were meeting every few weeks to talk about my research. One day in passing he mentioned that he was organizing a meeting with some local foundation professionals to learn from leading scholars of religion, ethnicity, and education. "Boy, would I love to be a fly on the wall of that meeting!" I said, and a week later he made it happen. One of the people at the meeting was Christian Smith, a sociologist at Notre Dame. He told the group about his recent project, the National Study of Youth and Religion (NSYR), a nationally representative survey and interview-based study that followed 3,290 American teens for ten years. He explained that the Jewish oversample had not been used much and said that if anyone happened to know graduate students looking for dissertation data, this might be a good option. I didn't know what I would do with the data, but I knew I could figure it out. This one meeting shaped the course of my entire research agenda.

Of course, conferences can be intimidating and overwhelming for people who are more introverted. But as Bruce points out, "Part of being entrepreneurial is trying to do something with my ideas and that requires starting conversations from a place that may feel unfamiliar or uncomfortable." Tied to that idea about uncomfortable conversations is a willingness to take the plunge and try meeting people who are outside one's field of interest. The ramifications of having conversations across disciplines reach far beyond just idea generation. Teresa Mangum, who has held several leadership roles thinking about the future of the humanities, argues that in the near future the single-author monograph will no longer be the main marker of success: "There are now whole fields that you just can't do well on your own. You need teams assembled. In fields like health humanities and environmental humanities, scientists and humanists have to work together to get anywhere"

Her point is plain: if academics don't generate ideas with others, they will be missing out on the next generation of research and publishing.

Funding and Community

The uncertainty of academia is hard to manage, but networks can help when confronted with high-risk situations or just experiencing a rough patch. For Narketta Sparkman-Key, now a vice provost and professor of education at James Madison University, her own network connected her to someone who turned out to be one of her greatest mentors. Key was pursuing her PhD online at Capella University when she ran out of funding. She had been trying to call different offices in the university to explain her situation and see if there was any way to fund the rest of her degree, but she was not making any progress. One day she posted to her Facebook group explaining her situation and received a very useful tip from a friend—the university had a program that they didn't advertise that might be a source of funding. "I called the office and a man answered and was like, 'We're gonna get you what you need.' He walked me through my entire program." For graduation, he even recorded a message telling Key how proud he was of her. "Sometimes mentors are strangers," Key says. "They're not people that we know or that we put in this place of saying 'are you up for being my mentor?'"

Nelson Zounlome aspired not only to leave graduate school debt free but also to start investing in a Roth IRA (an Individual Retirement Account that grows tax-free and allows you to withdraw your contributions and earnings tax-free after you reach age 59½) and a brokerage account (an investment account that allows you to buy and sell various types of securities, such as stocks, bonds, mutual funds, and exchange-traded funds). He knew that because of compounding interest, investing early in his life would help him have a more secure future. For Zounlome, who grew up in a low-income, single-parent household and lived in public housing most of his life, financial security was of paramount importance.[7] But how does a graduate student pay off debt *and* make enough money to invest?

While working on his PhD in counseling psychology at the University of Indiana, Zounlome wondered how he could draw on his own research and experience to help students of color navigate higher education. He started writing advice pieces and realized that he had the outlines of a book. That is how *Letters to My Sisters & Brothers: Practical Advice to Successfully Navigate Academia as a Student of Color* was born.[8] Zounlome also founded Liberate the Block, an organization that provides educational and mental health resources for BIPOC students. To start his business and publishing company, Zounlome leveraged all that his university had to offer—which surprisingly included access to lawyers, business planners, and financial advisors.

Leveraging his network enabled Zounlome to take ownership of his graduate education, to graduate debt free, secure over $200,000 in grants and fellowships (including the McNair Scholars Program and the Ford Foundation), and ultimately secure a tenure-track position in the Department of Educational, School and Counseling Psychology at the University of Kentucky.

Applying for grants and fellowships can also be a way to broaden one's community. One of the key ingredients of a compelling grant application is connecting your research and career goals to the mission of the organization. Instead of focusing on what he would gain and achieve through the award, José Riera studied closely the goals of the organizations and explained why they were important to him and how he could help the organization achieve them.

In this regard he was following the advice of Sophia Donaldson, a careers consultant for University College London: "You are the person with the ideas, but you have to convince people to fund your idea," she told me. In her own op-ed encouraging scholars to think like entrepreneurs, Donaldson encourages academics to hone their selling skills: "No matter if you're pitching for business funding or research funding, whether you're marketing your product to customers, or yourself to fellowship committees, all are exercises in sales. And any good salesperson knows the customer is crucial in the sales process. Get to know their needs and motivations, and you'll know your sales strategy."[9]

Vicki Johnson, founder and director of ProFellow, the world's leading online resource for professional and academic fellowships, also recommends speaking to at least three former fellows about the application process—which is another way to connect to other academics.[10] Some may even offer to share the application materials. And of course, you should look for funding opportunities outside the traditional grant route, which also offer chances to broaden your network. At Indiana, Eddie Cole found he could earn $1,000 by proposing a class, developing a syllabus, and then teaching it for part of the semester. Riera discovered research grants and scholarships that came from places that one would not traditionally think to look—like from the Washington State Employees' Credit Union, where he was a member.

Asking for money or help can be intimidating, as it involves the risk of rejection or imposing on others. Scholars, in particular, may hesitate to seek assistance due to fears of being turned down or criticized. However, as Steven Zhou, who has experience in the start-up world, points out, entrepreneurs often have a different perspective on rejection. They are accustomed to hearing "no" regularly and are able to move on without taking it personally. This resilience and ability to persevere despite setbacks can be a valuable mindset for academics as well.

Eddie Cole approached the fellowship and grant application process with a mindset similar to that of a baseball player: "If you bat .300, you get a hit three out of every ten, and that's [what] I had to think about academia. These things are time consuming, and you practice and say, 'Wow, I did all that practice, and I got one hit today.' You know, that is actually not bad." Entrepreneurs are comfortable with failure and keeping their nose to the grindstone, knowing that they will eventually hear yes from someone. Additionally, many fellowships offer the opportunity to reapply and provide feedback on rejected applications, enabling applicants to improve their future submissions.

During his time in graduate school, Cole secured over $20,000 in additional grants beyond his stipend. He utilized these funds for living expenses, conference travel, and research costs. José Riera, on the other hand, found his niche with grants ranging from $2,500 to $5,000. His success rate was impressive, as he applied for twenty-two different grants and was awarded eighteen of them. This demonstrates the importance of identifying the types of grants that best suit one's needs and focusing efforts on those opportunities.

Side Hustles and Community

The entrepreneurial mindset scholars adopt regarding academia's financial aspects is crucial. On the one hand, you can view yourself as an underpaid employee, exploited and undervalued, leading to a reluctance to engage in nonmandatory activities such as seminars and social events. As a result, you might miss out on crucial opportunities for learning and developing the community that can sustain you through the hardships you are experiencing.

On the other hand, you can adopt a more positive mindset. You can see your studies as a chance to learn at the university's expense, recognizing that despite a modest stipend, the university is investing significant resources in your education.[11] You can view any debt incurred as an investment in your future, enabling you to pursue careers with better long-term prospects. Most importantly, you can use your education to start thinking like an entrepreneur and take control of your financial situation.

Side hustles offer benefits beyond merely paying the bills. They help you discover your identity beyond professional achievements and allow you to assess your skills and explore different career paths. In the uncertain landscape of academia, side hustles encourage the development of practical skills relevant to your desired work, which can be transferred to other opportunities if a tenure-track position is not in your future. They also provide a means of building a community that can support your career progression.

When Erika Moore Taylor was choosing where to get her degree in biomedical engineering, a school's cost of living was a key consideration.[12] With $65,000 in undergraduate debt, she prioritized programs in areas with a lower cost of living. Her National Science Foundation Graduate Research Fellowship, combined with her choice to attend Duke University, allowed her to live above the living wage. By working as a graduate resident, she managed to pay off her student loans and gain valuable experience as a Professional Young Trustee at Duke.[13] This experience was an asset when she entered the job market, contributing to her becoming an assistant professor of materials science and engineering at the University of Florida and founding a financial literacy nonprofit.

One challenge to pursuing income-generating side projects is navigating the expectations and policies of advisors and departments. Not all advisors support students' side hustles, believing that graduate students should dedicate themselves fully to academia. However, if side projects advance your career, it's worth making the case to your advisor. For example, when Zounlome shared his desire to write a book for BIPOC scholars, his advisor was supportive because it aligned with his research. In contrast, when I decided to teach a sociology course at a community college, one of my advisors was less enthusiastic, feeling that my focus should be solely on research. Despite this, I proceeded with my plan, valuing their perspective but not letting it deter me. Looking back, I have no regrets, as the experience equipped me with skills that research alone could not provide.

Side hustles also enable you to expand your community beyond academia. José Riera's work outside his department led to a competitive summer internship with the Urban Leaders Fellowship, where he worked on Tennessee Department of Education projects related to student equity and special education. Although this wasn't his initial focus, his research experience and encouragement from his dissertation mentors led him to pursue opportunities aligned with his personal mission. This fellowship broadened his career options, and after completing his PhD, he was invited to collaborate with lower-income Hispanic and Native American agricultural communities in the greater Yakima Valley, combining his interests in education and business administration.

Nneka Dennie's diverse experiences during graduate school played a crucial role in expanding her skill set and perspectives, providing her with access to professional development opportunities and communities beyond the narrow purview of traditional humanities doctoral programs. Her roles ranged from substitute teaching and assisting a theater professor to working full-time as a program coordinator at a university women's center. These positions allowed her to explore various career paths outside academia, enabling her to detach from the conventional academic success narrative while still pursuing her doctorate.

The skills Dennie developed in these roles were not only relevant to her field but also transferable to other sectors. For instance, her work at the women's center allowed her to connect Black feminist theory with practice and explore innovative teaching methods for women's activism. She organized workshops, coordinated a Black feminist symposium, and even taught a course. Working full-time as a program coordinator for a year helped Dennie develop a healthy academic identity, realizing that "I am not defined entirely by my degrees. Having a side hustle made me divest my worth from my scholarly productivity. Research is what we do, but it is not who we are."[14]

Ultimately, Dennie pursued a tenure-track position in the history department at Washington and Lee University, confident in her decision to enter the job market because of the safety net her diverse experiences had provided. Her story highlights the value of exploring varied roles during graduate school not just as a means of financial support, but as a way to broaden one's skill set, perspectives, and career possibilities beyond academia.

Our worth as scholars and individuals extends beyond our academic achievements. Embracing diverse experiences and skills can lead to a more fulfilling and versatile career, reminding us that we are defined not solely by our degrees but by the breadth of our experiences and the impact we make in the world.

I want to acknowledge that pursuing side hustles comes with its own set of challenges, particularly for certain groups of students. International students, for example, often face visa restrictions that limit their ability to engage in income-generating activities outside their studies. Students with care-taking responsibilities, either for their children or for other family members, may find it difficult to balance their academic commitments with the demands of a side hustle. The time and energy required to manage both can be overwhelming, leading to increased stress and potential burnout. Institutions can certainly do more to provide flexible and supportive policies that accommodate the diverse needs and circumstances of their students.

Why It Matters

Narketta Sparkman-Key has continually relied on mentors to navigate difficult moments of her career, including a series of challenges that arose during her tenure review. "I have all kinds of mentors and they have taught me all kinds of things, giving me all kinds of insights. They have diverse perspectives and they have had different trajectories and journeys, and they've seen different things. That really helps me." Mentors can also provide emotional support by listening to your concerns, empathizing, and offering advice. As Gladys Ato recalls, one of her mentors offered support when she most needed it. "Somebody told me I could do it. I needed that permission." She went on to observe that "when you invest in a mentor, you are able to get a roadmap presented to you. But equally important is having somebody say, 'you can do this' which becomes really valuable when we are so used to having been told what to do."

Scholars should recognize that building community can help other academics and recognize the value they themselves bring to relationships. As art history professor Susan Sidlauskas writes, "Your presence matters to others. By the time you are in your second or third year of study, you are living, breathing proof to rookie students that there is life beyond those exams; that in fact, actual human beings who look and sound a bit like them—only smarter—have come up with dissertation topics. They will think to themselves, 'perhaps I could do that, too.'"[15]

Stacy Torres, a professor at University of California, San Francisco, exemplifies what it looks like to see yourself as part of an academic community and leverage your wisdom, especially when your family is not able to be a resource. Torres's mother died while she was in high school, and her father, who had immigrated to the US and whose English wasn't strong, couldn't help her navigate higher education. One of Torres's most influential mentors was a professor at Fordham University, where Torres went to undergrad. She encouraged Torres to pursue sociology. "I'm still receiving nuggets of wisdom from people who are ahead of me, including my own undergraduate advisor, who learned so much from her own mentors. It's nice to have this lineage of women passing on academic wisdom." Torres's comparative literature professor at Fordham was also deeply influential, helping Torres think about her future career, encouraging her to write, and helping her see that social justice was a key aspect of her work. In the tapestry of academia, mentorship emerges as a golden thread, weaving through the fabric of scholarly life with transformative grace.

Torres's journey at Fordham is a testament to this. Her professors, acting as cartographers of the academic landscape, charted a course for her future, infusing her pursuits with a sense of purpose and direction. They didn't merely impart knowledge; they kindled a fire within her, illuminating the path where social justice and scholarship converge.

Grateful for the mentorship she received, Torres now actively mentors younger students: "I try to take the responsibility to help people who are a few years behind me on their journeys as much as I can. As a first-gen student, I can find it hard to figure out some things that might seem basic to a lot of people, so at every stage, when I figure out something, I like to share that information." When Torres was in her first faculty position at SUNY Albany, she mentored graduate students who worked with her as research and teaching assistants. Some of these relationships translated to collaboration— including an op-ed in the *New York Times* about grandparents and immigration.

When we leverage our resources, remember that the journey of scholarship is not a solitary endeavor, but a community sport. Here are the key points to keep in mind:

Scholarship as a community: Just as entrepreneurs thrive on collaboration, scholars too benefit from engaging with a diverse network of peers, mentors, and professionals. Building relationships and exchanging ideas with others can (and typically will) enrich your research, provide support, and open up new opportunities. Embrace the collaborative nature of academia and seek out connections that can help you grow as a scholar.

Where to look for community: Finding your community can happen in various places, from conferences and seminars to online forums and interdisciplinary groups. Don't limit yourself to your immediate academic circle. Reach out to scholars in different fields, connect with professionals outside of academia, and seek mentorship from those who have navigated similar paths. Remember, your community is not just for academic support but also for personal growth and inspiration.

Funding and community: Financial support is crucial in academia, and your network can play a significant role in helping you secure funding. Engage with mentors and peers to learn about grant opportunities, fellowship programs, and other funding sources. Find ways to formally and informally share your research goals with potential funders who align with your interests and values. Remember, every funding opportunity is also a chance to expand your community and collaborate with others who share your vision.

Side hustles and community: Side hustles can be more than just a financial necessity; they can also be a way to explore new interests, develop transferable skills, and build a diverse network. Whether it's teaching, consulting, or starting your own venture, a side hustle can provide valuable experiences that enrich your academic and professional journey. Moreover, it can connect you with people outside academia, broadening your perspective and opening up new paths for collaboration.

5

Disseminating Your Ideas

IN 2016, Will Fenton was a doctoral student at Fordham University, where he was writing a dissertation about Quakers. Fenton had won a research fellowship that let him access archival data at the Library Company of Philadelphia. While working on one of his chapters Fenton came across a pamphlet about the 1763 Paxton massacre, where a group of backcountry vigilantes murdered twenty unarmed Susquehannock Indians. A month later, hundreds of these "Paxton boys" marched toward Philadelphia with plans to harm refugee Indians. Supporters and critics spent the year battling in a pamphlet war that resembles today's Twitter wars. Fenton realized that there was an abundance of pamphlets that had never been analyzed, and that there were other relevant printed materials that circulated contemporaneously.

The Paxton pamphlets and ancillary materials were not central to Fenton's dissertation, but he became enthralled by them. He wanted to share them with other scholars, but he didn't know how to do this. Then Fenton had an idea: What if he just asked the Library Company and the neighboring

Historical Society of Philadelphia to digitize all their Paxton holdings? The boldness was absurd—asking two prominent Philadelphia cultural heritage institutions to digitize hundreds of pages of materials at their own expense. But what did he have to lose? And as it turned out, both institutions were bringing on interns, and told Fenton that if he could define the task, the interns could help carry it out.

Over the next several months, Fenton worked with the librarians to identify the appropriate materials and collect metadata in a shared database. He spent countless hours working with technologists at both institutions, learning about preservation plans, developing standardized scanning protocols, and crafting a memorandum of understanding (MOU) that stipulated the roles and responsibilities of all parties.

But once the interns digitized the materials, Fenton had to figure out how to make the material discoverable. How do you tell a story, he wondered, of a colonial massacre, mediated through colonial documents, in a manner that doesn't simply reproduce colonial biases, assumptions, and erasures? What might it look like to tell a story about the Conestoga, their fortitude, and their formative role in the history of colonial Pennsylvania? Fenton collaborated with the Library Company to coauthor a major grant application called "Redrawing History: Indigenous Perspectives on Colonial America," which was ultimately funded by the Pew Center for Arts & Heritage.

And once Digital Paxton launched in 2017, Fenton presented in multiple venues so that other scholars and the general public would learn about this new resource. He even participated in Archives Month Philly, where scholars go out and do public humanities. Fenton got assigned to the Frankford beer hall to talk about his project. He had no slides and no paper to read—just a mic, a beer, and an audience of 150 people at various stages of inebriation. "It was daunting. But you start to learn how to read the audience, you see what they're responding to, and you amplify particular components. You have to make adjustments on the fly. But afterward, I had a line of people asking for my contact information so they could learn more about what I was doing. And these are just people hanging out at a beer hall on a Thursday night in Fishtown!"

As a result of these presentations and the contacts he made, Fenton discovered troves of new material that could be added to the database. Today, Digital Paxton features materials from two dozen research libraries, archives, and cultural heritage institutions as well as contextual and interpretive materials from educators, historians, art historians, and literary scholars.

Will Fenton and the story of Digital Paxton is just one example of a larger point I want to make: that researchers and the world would benefit from zooming out of the nitty-gritty of research and contemplate how it connects to the world around them. Instead of hoarding their knowledge for just a select few in their field that can understand it, an entrepreneurial mindset sees knowledge production as an opportunity for ideas not just to grow but also to spread. The challenges scholars address are not solely their own; sharing solutions or even just insights can have a significant impact, guiding others toward refining these ideas and developing new, improved solutions to similar problems. By contributing to the broader discourse, scholars can help others overcome obstacles and advance their own work.

What Ideas Are For

What do you do with an idea? A popular children's book with that title tells the story of a child who has an idea.[1] "Where did it come from? Why is it here? What do you do with an idea?" the child wonders. At first, the child doesn't think much of his idea. He thinks it's strange and fragile. He worries what others will think and say about his idea. The idea follows him, but he acts like it doesn't belong to him. He keeps it to himself. He hides it and doesn't talk about it. He tries to act like everything is the same before his idea showed up.

Slowly, the child starts to realize that there is something magical about his idea. He feels better and happier when it is around but realizes that his idea needs to be nourished. It wants food. It wants to play. It wants attention. As he sustains his idea, it grows bigger. Feeling more confident, the boy decides to show it to other people, even though he is afraid. What if they laugh at it or think it is silly? And you know what? Many of them did laugh. They said the idea was no good. It was too weird. It was a waste of time. It would never become anything.

At first, the child believes them. He thinks about giving up on his idea. Then he realizes something: it's okay if his idea is different and weird. It's okay if it's a little crazy. Rather than giving up on it, the child continues to give his idea attention. He cares for it, feeds it, works with it, and plays with it. He even builds a house for his idea—a house with an open roof where his idea could look up at the stars and be safe to dream. As his idea grows and grows, so does his love for it. Being with his idea makes the child feel alive. He feels like he can do anything. It encourages him to think big, and then to think even bigger.

His idea shares secrets with him. It shows him how to walk on his hands because, it says, it is good to have the ability to see things differently.

And then one day, something amazing happens. His idea changes right before his eyes. It spreads its wings, takes flight, and bursts into the sky. His idea goes from being here to being everywhere. It is no longer just a part of the child, but now a part of everything. The boy realizes what you do with an idea: you change the world.

Being an entrepreneurial scholar is not just a matter of developing expertise in your subject area. It's about the mindset that allows you to use your expertise to be a thought leader. Within the academy the key metrics of success include the quantity and quality of publications (especially the ranking of the journal or press it's published with), but measuring success based on citation or paper count doesn't necessarily translate to how influential an idea is. From an entrepreneurial mindset, who cares if there is a huge corpus of knowledge if it doesn't add any value to the human condition? Tamara Gilkes Borr offers a blunt assessment of chasing metrics: "No one in the real world cares if you fill a gap in the scholarly literature. We care about problems. There are plenty of extremely serious problems right now."

Certainly, the increasing demands on scholars to be productive and efficient (often taking on more service and teaching responsibilities) makes it hard to take time to translate their work so that it can be accessible and influential beyond the academy. Why should academics spend hours giving public talks or writing op-eds if universities don't reward them for doing so? Some scholars have gotten so frustrated with the incentive structure of academia that they left. Matt Welsh, for example, left his tenured position at Harvard because he wanted to have a broader impact on society and felt that too often academics weren't serving as thought leaders: "You have to communicate your ideas to people. What is your opinion? What is your vision? Many academics don't seem to have an opinion. They're content to just write the paper, but it's hard to say that they're a thought leader. But people who can articulate a vision and have an opinion and build a community around their ideas—those are thought leaders. Academic leadership is about being the person with the ideas and getting other people on board with your ideas. That's what makes you a thought leader as opposed to somebody who's just doing the work."

Navigating the public sphere is essential, regardless of whether one remains in academia. BIPOC scholars, particularly those focusing on inequality, view the role of thought leaders as a vital tool for improving the lives of marginalized groups. Taura Taylor, a sociologist at Morehouse College, highlights the importance of aligning research with social change: "Some scholars are content with pure research, but given our focus on societal inequalities, our work should aim for social change. We often write for our peers, but our research needs to reach the public sphere. We should see ourselves as vehicles for that change." Eddie R. Cole reflects on the historical context of Black scholars' public engagement: "Black scholars have long recognized the significance of commenting on social issues beyond academic confines. My work continues this tradition, not as something new, but as a vital part of being a Black thinker in America, especially in discussions about race." Gladys Ato stresses the importance of connecting with audiences: "Academic language often centers on facts, theories, and research, but we must not overlook the most important part—engaging our audience."

The path forward for graduate students and early career scholars with an entrepreneurial mindset is clear. If you want your ideas to address problems and change the world, you need to nourish those ideas. To play with them. To feed them. To see how they help people see things differently. And to do that, you need to write and talk about your ideas to different audiences. But how one does that entrepreneurially is different from the cultural expectations associated with academic writing.

When to Start Sharing

In the children's story told in the previous section, the child's idea is initially small. Entrepreneurs might think of an early idea as a minimum viable product (MVP)—an early product that has flaws. In the entrepreneurship world, people do not generally wait till their product is perfect. They start selling when the product is viable. Who buys these? Early adopters. People who love new gadgets. After securing initial customers, they ask them for feedback (which they sometimes take). Then they iterate the product's design and ship new versions constantly.

In the academic world, having an MVP approach to one's ideas can also be helpful. It's all about putting an idea out into the world and seeing how it lands. What kind of response does it generate? This helps figure out where to take the idea. This is precisely why presenting in seminars is helpful, but there are other ways to test your MVP. Can you write an op-ed before writing a full paper? Can you give a talk outside of academia? During graduate school I collected large amounts of survey and social network data that I planned to use to write a book, but I knew it would take years to do that. Even writing a paper would take years. But I also knew after conducting all the interviews and doing some preliminary analysis that there were interesting trends, so I wrote an article for *Inside Higher Ed*. There were several positives that came out of this—emails from other scholars and even the president of a university who reached out to tell me they appreciated me sharing my ideas along with a speaking gig with Heterodox Academy. I eventually wrote a paper using some of the ideas from the op-ed, but refining them through these other venues made a big difference.

Thinking of your writing in terms of MVP will certainly lead to you experiencing moments of self-doubt. David Labaree says that "one way to keep your neurotic self-doubt under control is to bear in mind an important guiding principle for good writing: you are under no obligation to provide a perfectly uncontestable story." The confidence to write isn't the same thing as the confidence that your analysis is completely rock solid. "You need to have enough logic and evidence supporting your account to make you reasonably confident that it's accurate, but you don't need to be absolutely certain. Yours is not the last word on the subject."

Labaree notes that there is another often unsaid virtue to not being entirely convinced of the logic of your analysis.

Embracing the uncertainty of your assertion will also make your writing more effective. It will save you from feeling compelled to qualify every statement and provide a counter to every argument, which will only cloud the clarity of your writing and undercut the urgency of the story you're telling. You want to produce an analysis that is razor-sharp, cutting through the issues cleanly—not one that is surrounded with so many hedges and equivocations that your point disappears from sight.

In other words, Labaree takes seriously the point of being in conversation with others. "Add a credible and provocative contribution, and let others provide counterarguments."[2]

Creativity and big-picture thinking are qualities we often associate with great entrepreneurs—people with the vision to create products we don't yet know we need. Researchers, however, more often display focused, methodical, logical thinking—an extreme dedication to the task at hand. Their ideas rarely take flight because they are busy nailing down every loose end. But this is the antithesis of creativity. As Charalampos Mainemelis explains, "What usually kills or blocks one's creativity is lack of courage to explore novel or countercultural ideas, paralyzing anxiety about one's performance, and premature rejection of one's insights as inadequate or not worthy of further elaboration."[3]

The only criterion for putting something out in print is whether or not it will be a useful addition to the discourse—not whether it will stand the test of time or shine like a jewel for all to see. Labaree's advice is clear: "If you wait until you're absolutely certain about the issue, it's likely to be too late; the conversation will have moved on, and it will be the worse off for the absence of your contribution." After all, as Labaree points out, "There are no perfect arguments wholly protected from correction by others. So relax. Better to aim to be usefully provocative than to be boringly correct."

Of course, there are good and bad ways of being provocative. Graduate students and early career scholars don't want to diminish their professional identity by just churning out anything. In an era where synthesizing information is privileged, the temptation might be to rush an idea into print simply because a synthesis can be made. Howard Gardner offered this word of caution:

> We live in an era where rewards come to those who can synthesize in a versatile way: provide a brief summary of a complex set of ideas; write a blog; give a TED talk; do an effective interview on radio, TV, or a podcast; create a stimulating tweet and marvel if it goes viral. But can such a quick and necessarily superficial synthesizer go deeper, provide more details, handle challenges, realize when a criticism is valid as opposed to being irrelevant or based on a fundamental misunderstanding? Only if the answer to these questions is "yes" would I deem such a person to be a legitimate synthesizer.

There's one final reason why an MVP approach to entering an academic conversation makes sense as a writing strategy. It offers a coherent motivation for writing.

Many academics struggle to find the motivation to write. Several books give advice to help people overcome common barriers and become more productive writers.[4] These books often contain technical tips and strategies, such as adopting a writing schedule, sticking to it, and writing during the allotted time. But these kinds of technical questions don't address the fundamental question of motivation.[5] Christian Smith, who has written several books, suggests that "writing productivity is not a technical problem. It is an existential problem." As Smith explains, "Motivation to write comes from feeling like you have something important to say. It's a real inner belief that has a driving power, that you have something that is valuable, and that the world needs to hear. And it's not currently being said, or it's not being said the right way, or it's not being sort of framed the right way."

Smith feels most productive when there is a conversation going on in the larger world that he thinks he can contribute to. "It's believing that whoever has the microphone now doesn't totally have the story right, or they don't have the right picture, and there is something missing that I want to add or something I want to correct." Writing comes easiest when he sees the gap in how the topic is being discussed and knows he can contribute. "It's a highly motivating energy to think I have something important to say. And the sooner it gets said, the better the world is." Smith acknowledges that this position might sound egotistical, but it has always motivated him. "Techniques matter, but without the confidence that what you say is important, none of the techniques will really help."

Who to Share With

Selling ideas starts with thinking about the audience. For Rob Lalka, that means considering what it means for someone to take the idea seriously. Entrepreneurs are asking potential customers to spend their money in a way they haven't done before because they think what's on offer can solve their problem. Writers are doing something quite similar: they are asking people to give their time and focus. As Labaree notes, doing so "puts a lot of pressure on you to come through on your promises. It better be good." For him the demand is both reasonable and motivating: "That's a useful kind of pressure for the writer—the need to write something that's not humdrum but eye-opening" for your audience.[6]

When you talk about your research to different audiences, it can help to know their problem, or in the language of entrepreneurs their "pain point." Entrepreneurs develop products by identifying the issues that people have. Think about the products that are within the room you are sitting in. Chances are, most of them were designed to solve some sort of human problem. Getting your ideas into the public realm comes from understanding the market of ideas that you are contributing to. Scholars often think of this as entering a scholarly conversation, but it is also useful to think about what conversations in the real world you might be able to inform with your research.

That's not to say that you have to be responding to the market. At the MVP stage, initial ideas prior to peer review don't need to be market conscious—indeed, from the perspective of effectual thinking, knowledge of market demand might actually constrain creativity rather than foster it. Not knowing the constraints might lead you to something different and innovative. IPods didn't fill a market need—Steve Jobs created that market. So did Howard Shultz when he started Starbucks. But both of these innovators were aware that there was a potential audience—a very large audience it turned out—for their ideas.

Gaining an audience for your writing involves not just finding a voice but ensuring that voice resonates with your intended readers. Entrepreneurs understand the importance of building a brand that makes them memorable and distinct from their competitors, drawing customers to their products or services. They achieve this by pinpointing their target audience, crafting a unique value proposition, and shaping a recognizable identity. While scholars might initially find these entrepreneurial concepts alien, they actually engage in similar practices when they set themselves apart in their academic writing. Consider the typical literature review and motivation section of a scholarly article—the aim is to highlight gaps in existing research and position oneself as the one who will address these overlooked areas. The challenge, as Labaree suggests, is not just in developing innovative ideas but in cultivating a distinctive voice that makes readers think, "Ah, this sounds like [the author]." It's about balancing the articulation of your ideas with the development of a unique voice that leaves a lasting impression on your audience.

Writers must not only craft compelling narratives but also articulate the significance of their work in accessible language. As Gardner advised, "Explain your enterprise in the most suitable terms and concepts. Describe what you have done, the evidence you've used, and the analytical tools you've employed." It's essential for writers to proactively bridge the gap between their work and their readers, rather than expecting the audience to decipher the importance of their research on their own. Have clear explanations, tailored to different audiences if necessary, to ensure that people understand the value and purpose of your work.

The ultimate challenge for you as a writer is to bring the knowledge and expertise you possess to outside audiences—to test its value for a larger purpose—and connect it to what your audience cares about and what problems motivate them.[7] Imagine you are a writer researching the New Orleans public school system, which moved to a fully-based charter school system after Hurricane Katrina. If you are writing for a teacher's labor union newsletter, you might focus on the implications of charter school reform on teachers. If you are writing for a daily newsletter for congressional staffers like *The Hill*, you might focus on the implications of charter schools for educational policy. If you are writing for a research methods outlet, you might focus on how a natural disaster provides an opportunity for a quasi-experimental study.

Research has a funny way of being highly influential if scholars help it find the right audience. For example, elected officials are mostly buyers in the marketplace of ideas. Their job is to be a good funnel for good and creative ideas from the community, including academics. Your research can inform real-world problems by informing policy—if policymakers know about it.[8] Sally Hudson was an economics professor at the University of Virginia when she decided to take matters into her own hands and run for the Virginia House of Delegates.[9] She was frustrated that she was unable to inform and improve policies based on her research, but now she is positioned to create policies that are based on the latest data. One example was an email she received from grad students at UVA's medical school that explained that children's vaccination standards in Virginia were out of date. This helped Hudson realize that mandating HPV vaccines only for young girls, but not for young boys, was inconsistent with the scientific evidence. As a result, her team began working on legislation to include boys in the HPV vaccine protocol.

Steve Zhou used the various audiences at Lunch Club, an AI superconnector that connects users with common interests and objectives, to practice communicating his research so he could increase the reach of his ideas. Zhou's conversations forced him to practice how he talks about his research to people outside of his field. "The reality is there's only so many people in your field, and even if you publish a big-name study, at the end of the day, if you're lucky, a handful of other faculty and students will read and cite it. But that's it. And I'd like to think that we're doing research because we think it actually matters, that we can actually help people with our ideas." Teresa Mangum sums up the issue perfectly: "I adamantly argue that we need to think about ways to connect the discoveries we make with needs and opportunities in the world. And that actually doing so means that you have to be more articulate and clearer when you're speaking to nonspecialists about specialists' work. That will only make you do that work better because you're forcing yourself into clarity."

In the vibrant marketplace of ideas, the art of selling is not just about transactions; it's about connection. Just as entrepreneurs persuade customers to invest in their innovations, you as a writer must convince readers to invest their time and attention. The pressure to deliver something of genuine value is intense, yet it's this very pressure that sharpens the writer's focus. For scholars, understanding the audience is akin to an entrepreneur identifying a customer's pain point. Every product in your room, every service you use, originated from a problem someone sought to solve. In academia, entering the scholarly conversation is important, but so is engaging with the broader world. Your research can illuminate real-world discussions, provided you understand where it fits in the grand tapestry of public discourse. This doesn't mean pandering to the market. Initial ideas, like the seedlings of innovation, need room to grow without the constraints of market demands. Just as the iPod and Starbucks expanded into new markets, groundbreaking academic work can expand the boundaries of knowledge.

To resonate with an audience, scholars must find their unique voice. This is not about shouting the loudest but about speaking with clarity and authenticity. A literature review is more than a summary; it's a declaration of purpose, a statement of intent. It's about saying, "Here's what's been done, and here's what's been overlooked. I'm here to bridge that gap." Your voice is your signature, the mark that says, "This is my contribution."

Ultimately, the challenge for you as a writer is to take your knowledge beyond the ivory tower and into the world at large. The reality is that the reach of research is often limited within its own field. By engaging with diverse audiences, scholars can extend the impact of their work, making it more relevant and useful to the wider world. Explaining the importance of your work in plain language is crucial. Don't expect your audience to come to you; reach out to them, articulate your ideas in ways they can grasp, and be prepared to do it again and again.

Avenues for Sharing

Entrepreneurs often talk about having a distribution strategy, which means coming up with different ways to disseminate products or services. They think about how to turn risk into probabilities by taking a portfolio approach to their distribution. Perhaps there are five types of audiences for their product, and each one requires a different calculation about the risk and potential benefit. Scholars also need to think about their distribution strategies outside the scholarly book or journal and the benefits that might accrue as a result of taking risks and spending time writing for different audiences.

For example, one of the most common alternative distribution channels for ideas is through op-eds or articles that explain an issue in lay terms. Dalton Conley justifies writing op-eds because he sees their function as another form of teaching. "As I write up an op-ed, I try to tilt the frame that people view issues through. My motivation is to get people to think about an issue differently, not to proselytize for a particular position. I'm doing what I exactly try to do in an undergraduate class, but just for a wider audience." Some people tell him that writing an op-ed doesn't count as "real" idea sharing: "I agree that it's not research. It's not on the research ledger—it is meant to be on the teaching ledger. It's a form of public intellectual work as a form of teaching." Public writing can also yield many unexpected outcomes. Scholars I interviewed told me stories of how the public writing they did led to speaking invitations, funding opportunities, and even TED talks.

David Zvi Kalman also exemplifies the power of stepping out of the academic echo chamber. He regularly publishes articles for a public audience and embraces a philosophy of "public first." In his view, academics too often stop expecting people to respond to their work, letting them off the hook when it comes to thinking about what it looks like to package their ideas for a wider audience:

> Which conversation do you want to be part of? And where do you want to see impact? Is the impact you want that this vast wealth of knowledge gets a tiny bit bigger because twenty people read this paywalled article? Or do you actually just put your results out in public where everyone can see them?

It took a social connection to get him started with op-ed writing: "I was producing a podcast featuring Mark Oppenheimer, a journalist. I mentioned to him that I had this idea for an article about how the patent office is a repository of Jewish innovation. He was intrigued and helped me place it. That became the first public piece I ever wrote for Tablet Magazine." From there, Kalman started writing regularly for *The Forward*, *Tablet*, *Slate*, the *LA Times*, and *Haaretz*. "Working with people who are better networked than me has been very helpful in making those links and figuring out collaborations down the road."

Scholars can also disseminate their work in creative ways by collaborating with the communities they feel connected to. Teresa Mangum had a student writing a dissertation about literature and body imagery. She supported the student's interest in translating her research into practice: the student created a photo essay and developed a week-long class workshop for junior high girls, where she taught photography techniques along with feminist theories of the body, and then had them document what their body felt like without taking a picture. The students then had an exhibit at a gallery downtown that was open to the whole community. Mangum says the feedback loop is important: "We want them not only to think, 'How can my research inform the work in the community, but how can my research be improved from what I learned in the community and with the community partner?'"

Sarah Benor's Urban Dictionary of Jewish Language, the Jewish English Lexicon (JEL), shows how scholarship can yield something beyond an organized written piece. JEL is a collaborative database of distinctive words that are used in the speech or writing of English-speaking Jews. It emerged from a class project in a course she was teaching called "American Jewish Language and Identity in Historical Context," where she asked students to contribute words that they heard from their friends or read online or in print, as well as definitions, example sentences, and source language. Because Jewish and non-Jewish social networks overlap, these words are not used exclusively by Jews. The words in this database stem from several languages of the Jewish past and present, including the Hebrew and Aramaic of ancient biblical and rabbinic texts, the Yiddish, Ladino, and Judeo-Arabic of centuries of Jewish life in "the old country," and the Modern Hebrew of contemporary Israel. Some are English words that certain Jews use in distinctive ways, and some are Yiddish-origin words that have become part of the English language. As a result of Benor's creative way of thinking about language and her ability to bring the right people together to collaborate on this, people from all around the world are learning about Jewish language through platforms like Twitter, TikTok, YouTube, and Instagram.

Nonwritten modes of scholarly communication oftentimes lead to unexpected insights that might not have been uncovered without them. Benor loves giving public talks because of the breadth of audiences she reaches. The day before we met, she had given a talk on Yiddish to a group of Holocaust survivors and another talk on Jewish names to a group of people from all over the world. "I love sharing knowledge outside of the ivory tower. It's an important part of being an academic, even though it's not what we are socialized into." She is cognizant of audiences' having different needs: her talks on Jewish languages for practitioners (like camps and educational institutions) look quite different than a talk she would give for an academic audience or a public audience (like synagogue members). But both audiences can lead to exciting new avenues of research.

Recently Benor was chatting with someone in the audience after a talk when she realized that the Iranian Jews she was talking to didn't know what languages their great-grandparents spoke. She realized that very little was known about Iranian Jewish languages. Benor convened a few other language scholars and community organizations and together they successfully applied for a grant from the Wikimedia foundation (which houses Wiki Tongues) to document three Iranian languages and three Jewish neo-Aramaic dialects. The talks that Tricia Bruce has given have also yielded unexpected opportunities. Someone who watched her talk ended up interviewing her for a documentary they were making, and other people have contacted her to act as a consultant or join a steering committee.

In the bustling bazaar of ideas, entrepreneurs consider their distribution strategy, a roadmap for spreading their products or services far and wide. They navigate the uncertain terrain of the market by taking a portfolio approach, weighing the risks and potential benefits for different audiences. Scholars, too, must adopt a similar mindset, exploring diverse channels beyond the traditional scholarly book or journal. Writing op-eds, engaging in public intellectual work, and embracing a "public first" philosophy can open doors to new opportunities and broaden the impact of their research.

As scholars venture into the public arena, they discover that their work can resonate with a wider audience, sparking conversations, inspiring change, and leading to unforeseen collaborations. The challenge is to find the right balance between academic rigor and accessibility—to package ideas in a way that captivates and enlightens. The journey from the ivory tower to the global stage is fraught with uncertainty, but it's also filled with the promise of new connections, new insights, and a deeper sense of purpose. In the end, it's not just about disseminating knowledge; it's about enriching the tapestry of human understanding, one idea at a time.

Why It Matters

Lucy Partman has long wondered how a commitment to public scholarship could take the notion of publicly disseminating scholarly ideas one step further beyond writing op-eds. How could knowledge be disseminated outside of written form: "Can we use knowledge produced in other ways? How can this knowledge have an impact on society? Are there other types of programs, even companies or entities to create based on or informed by our research?" As she points out, "The credentialing tenure-track publication has become a key concern of the academy. But the metrics of the academy are one thing, and the metrics of an entrepreneur tend to be very different." What is urgently needed—and what entrepreneurially minded graduate students and early career scholars can offer—is "a diverse portfolio of approaches, ways of operating, and types of knowledge to draw from and combine in new ways."

Partman's "Looking Lab" was the first course at Princeton to marry the visual arts and entrepreneurship. "There are no lectures, no textbooks, no 'content dump.' It's a laboratory. We're working together to ask questions, develop hypotheses, conduct experiments and create new tools." In the first half of the semester, students learn the skills of "close looking" and research the experience of close looking itself. The term "close looking" is borrowed from art history, but Partman is working to reimagine it. She believes it can be valuable in all fields for collaboration and innovation—"and as a life practice."[10] In the second half of the course, they work in teams as entrepreneurs to design new tools to help people engage with the visual world and each other. "It's not about bringing STEM to the humanities or the humanities to STEM," she said. "In the Looking Lab, we start with problems and bring together knowledge and methods from all different fields to develop new practices and solutions. The drawing part is borrowed from engineering and the visual arts, the lab notebooks students keep are like field journals anthropologists use, and so on."

As a graduate student, postdoc, and lecturer, Partman has been steeped in bringing entrepreneurship to the humanist's perspective. "Many of the skills scholars develop—finding gaps in markets, dealing with vast amounts of ambiguity, building things from scratch—are those common to entrepreneurs," Partman said. Academics would be well advised to follow their lead: "I deeply believe that graduate students and PhDs can be agents of innovation, change and leadership—inside and outside of academia."

In the practice of disseminating your ideas, remember that the journey of scholarship is not just about creating knowledge; it's also about sharing that knowledge with the world. Here are some key points to keep in mind:

What ideas are for: Ideas are meant to be shared, nurtured, and allowed to grow. They have the potential to change the world, but only if they are given the opportunity to spread and interact with others. Embrace the unique and sometimes unconventional nature of your ideas, and don't shy away from sharing them, even if they seem fragile or imperfect at first.

When to start sharing: Consider sharing your ideas early while they are still developing. This approach, akin to an entrepreneur's MVP (minimum viable product), allows you to test your ideas, receive feedback, and refine them over time. Don't wait for perfection; let your ideas evolve through interaction and feedback.

Who to share with: Consider your audience carefully. Understand their needs, interests, and pain points, and tailor your message to resonate with them. Whether it's fellow academics, policymakers, or the general public, identify who can benefit from your ideas and make an intentional and tailored effort to reach them. Develop your unique voice and be able to explain the importance of your work in plain language.

Avenues for sharing: Explore diverse channels for disseminating your ideas. Beyond traditional academic publications, consider writing op-eds, engaging in public intellectual work, or collaborating with communities connected to your research. Utilize social media platforms and public talks to reach a wider audience. Be open to creative and nontraditional modes of sharing, such as photo essays, workshops, or collaborative databases.

Conclusion

THIS BOOK IS an invitation to scholars at all stages to think outside the academic box—to break free from conventional academic confines and embrace an entrepreneurial mindset. In a landscape where traditional paths are increasingly uncertain, embracing an entrepreneurial mindset is not just advantageous but essential. Doing so equips you with the ability to navigate the uncertainties of academia and life and empowers you to create opportunities that (hopefully) leave a lasting impact.

Our journey began with a pivotal shift in perspective: from being a diligent student to becoming an entrepreneurial scholar. It's a transformation from passively absorbing knowledge to actively generating it. It's about having faith in your potential, even when the road ahead is murky. It's about taking the reins of your academic voyage, charting your own course, and reveling in the independence it brings.

We then explored the terrain of uncertainty, a familiar domain for any entrepreneur. Embracing unpredictability, seizing opportunities through action, and learning to fail forward are not just start-up strategies: they're indispensable tools for the contemporary scholar. We discovered that often the most groundbreaking ideas emerge from stepping out of academia's safe harbor into the uncharted waters where real-world challenges await creative solutions.

We then delved into the idea business. For scholars, as for entrepreneurs, ideas are the currency of success. Pinpointing problems worth solving, refining your research questions, and investing your passion into your work are the foundations of influential scholarship.

Next, we examined the importance of leveraging resources. Scholarship, like entrepreneurship, thrives on collaboration. Cultivating relationships, finding your community, and effectively utilizing funding are all part of the equation. Side hustles, often viewed as mere distractions, can actually be a rich source of inspiration and a means to build a diverse network.

Lastly, we discussed the dissemination of your ideas. The scholarly journey doesn't end with the creation of knowledge; it's about sharing that knowledge with the world. This means knowing when to start sharing (as soon as possible with the right kinds of people), identifying your audience, and choosing the best channels to ensure your ideas have the maximum impact.

———

Landon Schnabel's story exemplifies the essence of the entrepreneurial scholar. As a kid growing up in a working-class family, Schnabel was constantly coming up with ideas to solve people's problems and make some side money. His dad managed a small auto body shop and Schnabel thought there would be a demand for cold drinks, especially in the hot Arizona summers. So he and his brother bought a used soda machine and placed it in the waiting area. They spent $300 on the machine and found deals on soda, typically spending twenty-five cents or less per can but charging twice that, and they soon recouped the cost of the machine and turned a nice profit. Schnabel also noticed that kids at his school liked to buy candy from the vending machine and wondered if they would be willing to buy it from him instead at a lower cost. He started with some leftover Halloween candy and went from there.

He was always coming up with ideas for how to fill needs and make some money, from catering parties to painting rooms for friends' parents. Schnabel assumed he would follow in the footsteps of many family members who had started small businesses. But Schnabel also wanted to make a meaningful difference in people's lives and decided to train as a minister. Yet in seminary he started to see all sorts of problems with religious institutions: he witnessed incidents of domestic violence and child abuse in the seminary housing apartments and noticed women and sexual minorities constantly being marginalized. None of this aligned with his view of religion as a way to help the disenfranchised, so Schnabel started considering different career paths.

Ever since his first entrepreneurial foray as a child, Schnabel had been intrigued by the idea of studying why people behave the way they do. Realizing that he could make a career out of studying social behavior, Schnabel applied to several sociology PhD programs. Schnabel no longer wanted to promote religion, so he decided to study it instead. But coming from a small religious college with a master's in divinity and no re-search experience didn't make him an especially attractive candidate to doctoral school admissions committees. He got accepted to one school: Indiana University. And yet by the time Schnabel graduated he had over twenty publications, a dozen publication awards, and a book contract with a top press. How did Schnabel become one of the most prolific young scholars in his field?

Schnabel attributes his success to having an entrepreneurial mindset. In college, Schnabel had felt like an employee. "You get assigned tasks, you turn them in, and your job is done." But in graduate school, Schnabel got to design his own assign-ments. "You're no longer just doing stuff for someone else—you're doing something for yourself." Although Schna-bel didn't come from a family of academics or an undergradu-ate program with faculty engaged in active research, there was one thing he did understand: to produce knowledge as a graduate student, you have to take the initiative. "I had to fig-ure out the market for what I can provide. How can I make a contribution in a crowded space? And what skills do I need to do what I want?"

Rather than trying to identify a research topic by looking for gaps in the literature, he thought about the problems and puzzles he noticed in divinity school. Why did religion, which claimed to help people, seem to hurt women and sexual minorities? How did religion contribute to rather than ame-liorate inequality? Schnabel was also a voracious reader, con-suming literature in a wide range of fields. What did psycholo-gists have to say about religion, gender, and inequality? What about political scientists, economists, and historians? As he explained, "Sometimes ideas are not brand-new things. An idea can just be a connection between two things that people haven't seen before. I tried to identify concepts and connect them to each other in interesting ways."

Schnabel also leveraged his resources. "I was so excited that the university was paying me to be there to learn, and I constantly found new ways to take advantage of what was available." He took classes beyond what was required. "I didn't think of coursework as something I had to do as a student to get my degree. I thought about it as an entrepreneur who wants to invest in their business by getting additional training." For example, the lab for his statistics class would often end early so that the instructor could answer students' questions, but most students would just leave. Schnabel took advantage of the opportunity to have the instructor teach him how to do all sorts of things, even beyond the scope of the class. Schnabel also used his courses strategically to work on research papers that turned into early journal articles. He would ask if he could alter the requirements of the course; instead of doing the required term paper, he asked to work on a publishable research paper—about which he would request feedback throughout the semester.

Schnabel also treated scholarship as a community sport, recognizing that collaborating with others made his work much more satisfying. "I like to work with someone who has a completely different approach. I have no idea where we will end up. In these cases, different ideas come together, and often we generate something that is much more novel than I could have imagined on my own." He also was eager to share his findings beyond the academy, and started writing for different blogs, eventually publishing pieces in the *Washington Post* and *Scientific American*, and gave a TEDx talk.

Why Entrepreneurial Scholarship Matters

As we've discovered, the essence of being an entrepreneurial scholar is not confined to the boundaries of academia. It's a way of thinking that transcends disciplines and sectors—a mindset that sees opportunities where others see obstacles and finds solutions in the face of uncertainty. It's about crafting something remarkable out of limited resources, and being a beacon of innovation in a fog of ambiguity. Being an entrepreneurial scholar is not just about what you know, but how you apply that knowledge to make a tangible impact in the world.

By viewing challenges as opportunities, leveraging our unique skills and networks, and remaining adaptable in the face of change, we can forge new paths for ourselves and make a lasting impact. The journey of an entrepreneurial scholar is not about adhering to a set script; it's about writing your own story. It's about recognizing that success in academia and beyond isn't confined to a single path but is a rich, colorful tapestry woven from your unique experiences, skills, and ambitions. By adopting an entrepreneurial approach, you've equipped yourself with the tools to turn challenges into opportunities and to view limitations not as barriers but as catalysts for new ideas.

Writing this book has itself mirrored the entrepreneurial principles discussed within. Transforming a thousand-word op-ed into a 50,000-word manuscript demanded faith in my capabilities amidst unclear prospects. Choosing to dive in meant embracing uncertainty and capitalizing on the opportunity to address a compelling issue.

The process stretched me in unexpected ways and taught me invaluable lessons, including the importance of resilience. Acquiring the necessary data involved reaching out to countless new contacts across various fields, learning from rejections, and refining my approach. This journey not only expanded my network but also connected me with an academic community eager to engage with my ideas. Moreover, it broadened my audience significantly—from focusing initially on graduate students to addressing the needs of female, first-generation, low-income, and BIPOC scholars, and even mid-career and more senior academics.

This journey has ultimately exemplified the very essence of being an entrepreneurial scholar: seeing opportunities in challenges, drawing on your unique experiences, and making an impact beyond traditional academic boundaries. As you move forward, remember to think creatively, build meaningful relationships, and use your intellectual, human, and social capital to make a positive impact. The future is (always) uncertain, but with an entrepreneurial mindset, you're equipped to shape it.

ACKNOWLEDGMENTS

One of the highlights of this book for me was writing Chapter 4, where I explore the concept of scholarship as a team sport. In this chapter, I invite scholars to envision the academic realm as a vast, interconnected network. In this web, each node represents a person; each link, a potential for collaboration, shared insight, or mutual support. Success in this network does not solely spring from individual brilliance but from the ability to tap into the collective wisdom, experience, and resources of our scholarly community.

This book itself is a product of that collective wisdom. Each page reflects the shared knowledge and collaborative spirit that fuels our academic endeavors.

A special thanks goes to Sam Wineburg, whose "Writing for a Public Audience" class at Stanford sparked this entire project. Sam, your insistence on refining my ideas turned a simple class assignment into the core concept for this book. When I wavered on publishing my original op-ed after several rejections, you urged, "Don't let it die. There was good stuff in there." Thank you for not letting the idea wilt.

I am grateful to Peter Dougherty, who saw the potential for a book in a humble *Inside Higher Ed* article—thank you for having the vision for this project and entrusting me with its creation. Your vision set this project in motion.

Thank you, Matt Rohal, for shepherding this book with such care and enthusiasm. Navigating through your detailed and humorous margin notes was one of the highlights of editing this manuscript.

Olson Pook, your editorial talents made my ideas sparkle. I'm immensely thankful for your magic touch.

Thank you to Lenny Cassuto, Howard Gardner, James Van Wyck, Ben Domingue, and Chris Caterine—your insights steered me to the right resources, the right people, and the right strategies to breathe life into these pages.

Heartfelt thanks to Yochai Shavit, Marissa Thompson, Blaze Bowers, and Minha Khan for meticulously reviewing the full manuscript and providing invaluable feedback. And to Hannah Kober, Kim Kushner, Tamara Frankel, Bryan Oren, Andrew Ergas, Nadia Beider, Julie Golding, Rafa Kern—your feedback on early drafts was crucial.

Liz Mount and Landon Schnabel, my steady writing companions for over four years, have provided thoughtful feedback and emotional support that were instrumental. You helped me sharpen my thinking and gave me the courage to express ideas I hesitated to share.

I'm indebted to the forty-three generous academics and entrepreneurs who shared their time and stories for the interviews. Your experiences and reflections are the backbone of this book.

To my incredible husband, Robbie, and our children, Araya and Mikayla, who supported this book's journey in countless ways—I couldn't have done it without you. Araya and Mikayla, maybe the next book will have pictures, just for you.

And finally, to my parents, Cecilia and Michael (z"l) Straznik, who instilled in me the spirit of entrepreneurship. To this day, I cannot fathom how you managed to start a business in a new country where you barely spoke the language. You showed me that anything is possible—a lesson that has allowed me to live in a world of endless possibilities.

Here's to the collaborative spirit of scholarship—may we always remember that we achieve our best work when we work together.

APPENDIX

TABLE 1. Interviewee Demographics[1] (N=43)

Name	Professional Role	Doctoral Degree / Institution	Gender pronouns	First-gen/ Low income[2]	BIPOC
Alison Miller	Founder/owner, The Dissertation Coach	Clinical Psychology, University of Illinois at Chicago	she/her		
Brian Bergman	Assistant Professor of Management, Tulane University	Entrepreneurship, Indiana University	he/him	X	
Christian Smith	Professor of Sociology, University of Notre Dame	Sociology, Harvard University	he/him		
Constantina Katsari	Tech entrepreneur	History, University College London	she/her	X	
Dalton Conley	Professor of Sociology, Princeton University	Biology, New York University Sociology, Columbia University	he/him		
David Labaree	Emeritus Professor of Education, Stanford University	Sociology, University of Pennsylvania	he/him		
David Zvi Kalman	Scholar in Residence/ Director of New Media, Shalom Hartman Institute; owner Print-O-Craft Press and the KLMNOPS Art House	Near Eastern Languages and Civilizations, University of Pennsylvania	he/him		
Eddie R. Cole	Associate Professor of Higher Education and History, University of California Los Angeles	Higher Education, Indiana University	he/him		X

Elaine Howard Ecklund	Professor of Sociology, Department of Sociology, Rice University	Sociology, Cornell University	she/her	X	
Emily Roberts	Founder/owner Personal Finance for PhDs; podcast host	Biomedical Engineering, Duke University	she/her		
Eran Shor	Professor of Sociology, McGill University	Sociology, Stony Brook University	he/him	X	
Gladys Ato	Clinical psychologist; former university president; host of *Time Out!* podcast	Clinical Psychology; Baylor University	she/her	X	X
Heather Frederick	Former university dean; host of *The Happy Doc Student* podcast	Social and Developmental Psychology, Brandeis University	she/her	X	
Howard Gardner	Professor of Cognition and Education and Senior Director of Project Zero, Harvard University	Developmental Psychology, Harvard University	he/him	X	
James McLurkin	Senior hardware engineer at Google; former engineering professor	Computer Science, Massachusetts Institute of Technology	he/him		X
Jennifer Burns	Associate Professor of History, Stanford University	History, University of California Berkeley	she/her		
José Riera	University lecturer of entrepreneurship and finance; researching technology supports for first-generation and immigrant learners	Higher Education, Washington State University	he/him		X
Josh Ladon	Director of Education for the Shalom Hartman Institute of North America	Education, William Davidson School at Jewish Theological Seminary	he/him		

(*continued*)

TABLE 1. (*continued*)

Name	Professional Role	Doctoral Degree/Institution	Gender pronouns	First-gen/Low income[2]	BIPOC
Karen Kelsky	Founder and president of The Professor Is In; former department head	Cultural Anthropology, University of Hawai'i	she/her		
Ken Bain	President of Best Teachers Institute; former university provost and history professor	History, University of Texas at Austin	he/him		
Kimberly Gramm	Chief Innovation and Entrepreneur Officer, Tulane University	Educational Leadership and Administration, Texas Tech University	she/her		
Landon Schnabel	Assistant Professor of Sociology, Cornell University	Sociology, Indiana University	he/him	X	
Lucy Partman	Lecturer, Princeton University	Art and Archaeology, Princeton University	she/her		
Matt Welsh	Chief architect and AI startup founder; former professor of computer science	Computer Science, University of California Berkeley	he/him		
Melissa Fuster	Associate Professor, School of Public Health and Tropical Medicine, Tulane University	Food Policy and Applied Nutrition, Tufts University	she/her		X
Murad Sabzali	Founding partner and board director for CG Life	N/A	he/him	X	
Narketta Sparkman-Key	Professor of Education and Vice Provost for Strategic Initiatives and Global Affairs, James Madison University	Human Services, Capella University	she/her	X	X

Nate Clark	Founder of Konnected	N/A	he/him		
Kathryn Paige Harden	Professor of Psychology, University of Texas at Austin	Clinical Psychology, University of Virginia	she/her		
Rob Lalka	Professor of Business and Executive Director of Center for Entrepreneurship and Innovation, Tulane University	N/A		X	
Rosa Arriaga	Associate Professor, School of Interactive Computing, Georgia Institute of Technology	Psychology, Harvard University	she/her	X	X
Sarah Bunin Benor	Vice Provost and Professor of Contemporary Jewish Studies, Hebrew Union College	Linguistics, Stanford University	she/her		
Scott Cowen	President Emeritus and Professor of Business, Tulane University	Finance, George Washington University	he/him		
Sophia Donaldson	Careers consultant, University College London	Molecular Genetics, University of College London	she/her		
Stacey Torres	Assistant Professor, Social Behavioral Sciences, University of California San Francisco	Sociology, New York University	she/her	X	X
Steven Zhou	Doctoral candidate, Organizational Psychology, George Mason University	PhD in progress	he/him		X
Sue Reinhold	Founding and managing partner; North Berkeley Investment Partners	Social Anthropology, University of Sussex	she/they		

(*continued*)

TABLE 1. (*continued*)

Name	Professional Role	Doctoral Degree/Institution	Gender pronouns	First-gen/ Low income[2]	BIPOC
Tamara Gilkes Borr	US policy correspondent, *The Economist*	Education, Stanford University	she/her	X	X
Taura Taylor	Assistant professor, Morehouse College	Sociology, Georgia State University	she/her	X	X
Teresa Mangum	Professor, Gender, Women, and Sexuality Studies and English; Director, Obermann Center for Advanced Studies, University of Iowa	English, University of Illinois, Urbana-Champaign	she/her		
Tricia Bruce	Sociologist, researcher, former professor	Sociology, University of California Santa Barbara	she/her		
William Fenton	Associate Director at the Center for Spatial and Textual Analysis, Stanford University	English, Fordham University	he/him		
Yehuda Kurtzer	President, Shalom Hartman Institute	Jewish Studies, Harvard University	he/him		

[1] As of summer 2023.

[2] Refers to someone who was the first person in their family to graduate from college, or grew up low-income.

NOTES

Introduction

1. Sarasvathy (2005).
2. Calarco (2020); Weisbach (2021); Kelsky (2015).
3. Horwitz (2021).
4. Several recent books call for changes to graduate education, including Horinko, Reed, and Van Wyck (2021); Cassuto (2015).
5. *The Economist* (2010).
6. Townsend (2021).
7. Flanagan and Wright (2022).
8. Schuman (2013).
9. Bok (2015).
10. Dalgleish (2013).
11. Cassuto (2015).
12. Horinko, Reed, and Van Wyck (2021).
13. Lalka (2024).
14. Berg and Seeber (2016).
15. Berg and Seeber (2016).
16. Rohrbach (2021).
17. Neck, Neck, and Murray (2018).
18. Stevens, Miller-Idriss, and Shami (2018).
19. Labaree (2017; 2018).
20. Labaree (2018).
21. Labaree (2017; 2018).
22. Sarasvathy (2005).
23. Miller (2008).
24. Sarasvathy (2008).
25. Levitt (2022a).

26. Lord (2021).
27. Horinko, Reed, and Van Wyck (2021), emphasis added.
28. Reyes (2022).
29. Rohrbach (2021).
30. Mullen, Goyette, and Soares (2003); Dam (2022).
31. Schultz and Stansbury (2022).
32. Dam (2022).
33. Calarco (2020).
34. Wanzer-Serrano (2022).
35. Bellemare (2022); Furstenberg (2013); Calarco (2020); Weisbach (2021); Haggerty and Doyle (2015); Cassuto (2015); Miller (2008); Frederick (2022); Zounlome (2020); Mullaney and Rea (2022),

1. An Entrepreneurial Mindset

1. Bankoff (2016).
2. Bankoff (2016).
3. Kerr, Kerr, and Xu (2018); Brandstätter (2011).
4. Conley (2018).
5. Posselt (2018).
6. Furstenberg (2013, 5).
7. Furstenberg (2013, 29).
8. Gracey (1975).
9. Levitt (2020).
10. Furstenberg (2013, 74).
11. Lange (2012); Grünhagen et al. (2014); Gelderen (2016).
12. Weisbach (2021, 18).
13. Cassuto and Van Wyck (2021).
14. Cassuto (2021).
15. Gardner (2020).
16. Gardner (2020).
17. Gardner (2020).
18. Calarco (2020).
19. Wanzer-Serrano (2022).
20. Bravata et al. (2020).
21. Ahmed et al. (2020); Vaughn, Taasoobshirazi, and Johnson (2019); Pulliam and Gonzalez (2018); Chakraverty (2022); Standlee (2018); Zounlome (2020).

22. Hall and Arneman (2022).

23. Bandura (2009).

24. Nori and Vanttaja (2022).

25. Walkington (2017); Holmes et al. (2022)

26. Sparkman-Key (2021).

2. Navigating Uncertainty

1. Burns (2009).

2. Cassuto (2013); Ph.D. Completion Project (2007).

3. Neck, Neck, and Murray (2018).

4. Neck, Neck, and Murray (2018); Taghavi (2018).

5. Lane (2012).

6. Fletcher and Benveniste (2022).

7. Levitt (2022c).

8. Miller (2022).

9. Chambers (2021).

10. Martinez and Byrne (2023).

11. Henry (2013).

12. Deresiewicz (2015).

13. Donaldson (2018).

14. Dweck (2008).

15. Ries (2011).

16. Neck, Neck, and Murray (2018).

17. Gerard (2021).

18. Shakha (2014).

19. Wood (2013).

20. Wood (2019).

21. Cassuto (2021).

22. Cassuto (2021).

23. McAdams (2008); McAdams et al. (1997).

3. The Idea Business

1. Swaminathan (2012).

2. Alon (2009).

3. Weisbach (2021, 200).

4. Sidlauskas (2017)
5. Weisbach (2021).
6. Dalgleish (2013).
7. Levitt (2022b)
8. Levitt (2022b).
9. Levitt (2022a)

4. Leveraging Resources

1. Roberts (2022).
2. Neck, Neck, and Murray (2018).
3. Lewis (2016).
4. Tello-Trillo and Hollingsworth (2020).
5. Dennie (2018b).
6. Dennie (2018b).
7. Roberts (2021b).
8. Zounlome (2020).
9. Donaldson (2018).
10. Johnson (2018).
11. Yale Graduate School of Arts and Sciences (2024).
12. Roberts (2021a).
13. Duke University (2017).
14. Dennie (2018a).
15. Sidlauskas (2017).

5. Disseminating Your Ideas

1. Yamada (2014).
2. Labaree (2021).
3. Mainemelis (2001).
4. Belcher (2019); Sylvia (2018).
5. For a great resource on this, see Sword (2023).
6. Labaree (2021).
7. Rohrbach (2021).
8. Badgett (2017).
9. Tello-Trillo and Hollingsworth (2021).
10. Saxon (2022).

REFERENCES

Ahmed, Afran, Tatyana Cruz, Aarushi Kaushal, Yusuke Kobuse, and Kristen Wang. 2020. "Why Is There a Higher Rate of Impostor Syndrome Among BIPOC?" *Across the Spectrum of Socioeconomics* 1, no. 2. https://doi.org/10.5281/zenodo.4310477.

Alon, Uri. 2009. "How to Choose a Good Scientific Problem." *Molecular Cell* 3, no. 6: 726–728.

Badgett, M. V. Lee. 2017. *The Public Professor: How to Use Your Research to Change the World*. New York: NYU Press.

Bandura, Albert. 2009. "Cultivate Self-Efficacy for Personal and Organizational Effectiveness." In *Handbook of Principles of Organizational Behavior: Indispensable Knowledge for Evidence-Based Management*, 2d ed., edited by Edwin Locke, 179–200. Hoboken, NJ: Wiley.

Bankoff, Caroline. 2016. "How Selling Fax Machines Helped Make Spanx Inventor Sara Blakely a Billionaire." *New York Magazine*, October 31. https://nymag.com/vindicated/2016/10/how-selling-fax-machines-helped-sara-blakely-invent-spanx.html.

Belcher, Wendy Laura. 2019. *Writing Your Journal Article in Twelve Weeks: A Guide to Academic Publishing Success*, 2nd ed. Chicago: University of Chicago Press.

Bellemare, Marc F. 2022. *Doing Economics: What You Should Have Learned in Grad School—But Didn't*. Cambridge, MA: MIT Press.

Berg, Maggie, and Barbara K. Seeber. 2016. *The Slow Professor: Challenging the Culture of Speed in the Academy*. Toronto: University of Toronto Press.

Bok, Derek. 2015. *Higher Education in America*. Princeton, NJ: Princeton University Press.

Brandstätter, Hermann. 2011. "Personality Aspects of Entrepreneurship: A Look at Five Meta-Analyses." *Personality and Individual Differences* 51, no. 3: 222–230.

Bravata, Dena M., Sharon A. Watts, Autumn L. Keefer, Divya K. Madhusudhan, Katie T. Taylor, Dani M. Clark, Ross S. Nelson, Kevin O. Cokley, and Heather K. Hagg. 2020. "Prevalence, Predictors, and Treatment of Impostor Syndrome: A Systematic Review." *Journal of General Internal Medicine* 35, no. 4: 1252–1275.

Burns, Jennifer. 2009. *Goddess of the Market: Ayn Rand and the American Right.* New York: Oxford University Press.

Calarco, Jessica M. 2020. *A Field Guide to Grad School: Uncovering the Hidden Curriculum.* Princeton, NJ: Princeton University Press.

Cassuto, Leonard. 2013. "Ph.D. Attrition: How Much Is Too Much?" *Chronicle of Higher Education,* July 1. https://www.chronicle.com/article/ph-d-attrition-how-much-is-too-much/.

———. 2015. *The Graduate School Mess: What Caused It and How We Can Fix It.* Cambridge, MA: Harvard University Press.

———. 2021. "Foreword: Toward a Sustainable Future." In *The Reimagined PhD: Navigating 21st Century Humanities Education,* edited by Leanne M. Horinko, Jordan M. Reed, and James M. Van Wyck, ix–xi. New Brunswick, NJ: Rutgers University Press.

———, and James Van Wyck. 2021. "The PhD Adviser-Advisee Relationship Reimagined for the Twenty-First Century." In *The Reimagined PhD: Navigating 21st Century Humanities Education,* edited by Leanne M. Horinko, Jordan M. Reed, and James M. Van Wyck, 42–54. New Brunswick, NJ: Rutgers University Press.

Chakraverty, Devasmita. 2022. "Impostor Phenomenon Among Hispanic/Latino Early Career Researchers in STEM Fields." *Journal of Latinos and Education* 23, no. 1: 250–268.

Chambers, Paula. 2021. "Afterword: From Action to Collective Action." In *The Reimagined PhD: Navigating 21st Century Humanities Education,* edited by Leanne M. Horinko, Jordan M. Reed, and James M. Van Wyck, 176–190. New Brunswick, NJ: Rutgers University Press.

Conley, Joseph. 2018. "Just Another Piece of Quit Lit." *Chronicle of Higher Education,* March 8. https://www.chronicle.com/article/just-another-piece-of-quit-lit/.

Dalgleish, Melissa. 2013. "My 'I Quit' Letter." *Hook & Eye,* November 7. https://hookandeye.ca/2013/11/07/my-i-quit-letter/.

Dam, Andrew Van. 2022. "People from Elite Backgrounds Increasingly Dominate Academia, Data Shows." *Washington Post,* July 8. https://www.washingtonpost.com/business/2022/07/08/dept-of-data-academia-elite/.

Dennie, Nneka D. 2018a. "Always Have a Side Hustle, and Other Lessons I Learned from Academia." The Professor Is In, guest post, August 12. https://the professorisin.com/2018/08/12/always-have-a-side-hustle-and-other-lessons -i-learned-from-academia-guest-post/.

———. 2018b. "Always Have a Side Hustle, and Other Lessons I Learned from Academia (Part 2)." The Professor Is In, guest post, August 25. https:// theprofessorisin.com/2018/08/25/always-have-a-side-hustle-and-other -lessons-i-learned-from-academia-part-2/.

Deresiewicz, William. 2015. *Excellent Sheep: The Miseducation of the American Elite and the Way to a Meaningful Life*. New York: Free Press.

Donaldson, Sophia. 2018. "Academics as Entrepreneurs." The Professor Is In, guest post, July 13. https://theprofessorisin.com/2018/07/13/academics-as -entrepreneurs-guest-post/.

Duke University. 2017. "Duke Adds Six New Members to Board of Trustees." July 19, *Duke Today*. https://today.duke.edu/2017/07/duke-adds-six-new-members -board-trustees.

Dweck, Carol S. 2008. *Mindset: The New Psychology of Success*. New York: Random House.

Flanagan, Christopher, and Glenn Wright, eds. 2022. *Leaving the Grove: A Quit Lit Reader*. Syracuse, NY: The Graduate School Press, Syracuse University.

Fletcher, Angus, and Mike Benveniste. 2022. "A New Method for Training Creativity: Narrative as an Alternative to Divergent Thinking." *Annals of the New York Academy of Sciences* 1512, no. 1: 29–45.

Frederick, Heather. 2022. *The Happy Doc Student Handbook: 7 Steps to Graduating with Your Sanity, Health, and Relationships Intact*. Chandler, AZ: Expand Your Happy!

Furstenberg, Frank F. 2013. *Behind the Academic Curtain: How to Find Success and Happiness with a PhD*. Chicago: University of Chicago Press.

Gardner, Howard. 2020. *A Synthesizing Mind: A Memoir from the Creator of Multiple Intelligences Theory*. Cambridge, MA: MIT Press.

Gelderen, Marco van. 2016. "Entrepreneurial Autonomy and Its Dynamics." *Applied Psychology* 65, no. 3: 541–567.

Gerard, Stephan. 2021. "Fail Fast and Fail Forward . . . Learn By Doing!" *Forbes*, July 29.

Gracey, Harry L. 1975. "Learning the Student Role: Kindergarten as Academic Boot Camp." In *School and Society: A Sociological Approach to Education*, edited by Jeanne H. Ballantine, Joan Z. Spade, and Jenny M. Stuber, 82–95. Thousand Oaks, CA: SAGE Publications.

Grünhagen, Marko, Melody L. Wollan, Olufunmilola Dada, and Anna Watson. 2014. "The Moderating Influence of HR Operational Autonomy on the Entrepreneurial Orientation–Performance Link in Franchise Systems." *International Entrepreneurship and Management Journal* 10, no. 4: 827–844.

Haggerty, Kevin, and Aaron Doyle. 2015. *57 Ways to Screw Up in Grad School: Perverse Professional Lessons for Graduate Students.* Chicago: University of Chicago Press.

Hall, Joshua, and Daniel Arneman. 2022. "Practical Advice for Overcoming Imposter Syndrome w/Dr. Maureen Gannon." Episode 71, December 31, in *Hello PhD*, podcast audio. https://hellophd.com/2022/12/071-practical-advice-for-overcoming-impostor-syndrome-w-dr-maureen-gannon-r/.

Henry, Erica. 2013. "7 Epic Fails Brought to You By the Genius Mind of Thomas Edison." *Smithsonian Magazine*, November 20. https://www.smithsonianmag.com/innovation/7-epic-fails-brought-to-you-by-the-genius-mind-of-thomas-edison-180947786/#:~:text=In%20response%20to%20a%20question,ways%20that%20will%20not%20work.%E2%80%9D.

Holmes, Oscar, Alexis Nicole Smith, Denise Lewin Loyd, and Angélica S. Gutiérrez. 2022. "Scholars of Color Explore Bias in Academe: Calling in Allies and Sharing Affirmations for Us by Us." *Organizational Behavior and Human Decision Processes* 173 (November): 104204. https://doi.org/10.1016/j.obhdp.2022.104204.

Horinko, Leanne M., Jordan M. Reed, and James M. Van Wyck, eds. 2021. *The Reimagined PhD: Navigating 21st Century Humanities Education.* New Brunswick, NJ: Rutgers University Press.

Horwitz, Ilana M. 2021. "Why Ph.D. Students Should Think Like Entrepreneurs." *Inside Higher Ed*, July 7. https://www.insidehighered.com/advice/2021/07/08/phd-students-will-be-more-successful-if-they-think-entrepreneurs-opinion.

Johnson, Vicki. 2018. "How to Win Competitive Fellowships: 5 Secrets of Fellowship Winners." ProFellow, February 15. https://www.profellow.com/tips/how-to-win-competitive-fellowships-5-secrets-of-fellowship-winners/.

Kelsky, Karen. 2015. *The Professor Is In: The Essential Guide to Turning Your Ph.D. Into a Job.* New York: Crown Publishing Group.

Kerr, Sari Pekkala, William R. Kerr, and Tina Xu. 2018. "Personality Traits of Entrepreneurs: A Review of Recent Literature." *Foundations and Trends® in Entrepreneurship* 14, no. 3: 279–356.

Labaree, David. 2017. *A Perfect Mess: The Unlikely Ascendancy of American Higher Education.* Chicago: University of Chicago Press.

———. 2018. "Higher Education in the US Is Driven by a Lust for Glory | Aeon Essays." Aeon. https://aeon.co/essays/higher-education-in-the-us-is-driven-by-a-lust-for-glory.

———. 2021. "Academic Writing as an Exercise in Arrogance and Humility." *Inside Higher Ed,* March 31. https://www.insidehighered.com/advice/2021/04/01/good-academic-writing-requires-both-arrogance-and-humility-opinion.

Lalka, Rob. 2024. *The Venture Alchemists: How Big Tech Turned Profits Into Power.* New York: Columbia Business School Publishing.

Lane, Terran. 2012. "On Leaving Academe." *Chronicle of Higher Education,* August 19. https://www.chronicle.com/article/on-leaving-academe/.

Lange, Thomas. 2012. "Job Satisfaction and Self-Employment: Autonomy or Personality?" *Small Business Economics* 38, no. 2: 165–177.

Levitt, Steven D. 2020. "Mayim Balik: 'I Started Crying When I Realized How Beautiful the Universe Is.'" September 4, in *People I (Mostly) Admire,* produced by Matt Hickey, podcast audio. https://freakonomics.com/podcast/mayim-bialik-i-started-crying-when-i-realized-how-beautiful-the-universe-is-people-i-mostly-admire-ep-2.

———. 2022a. "The Price of Doing Business, with John List." December 9, in *People I (Mostly) Admire,* produced by Morgan Levey, podcast audio. https://freakonomics.com/podcast/the-price-of-doing-business-with-john-list/.

———. 2022b. "Self-Help for Data Nerds." May 13, in *People I (Mostly) Admire,* produced by Morgan Levey, podcast audio. https://freakonomics.com/podcast/self-help-for-data-nerds/.

———. 2022c. "There's So Many Problems—Which Ones Can I Make a Difference On?" July 8, in *People I (Mostly) Admire,* produced by Morgan Levey, podcast audio. https://freakonomics.com/podcast/theres-so-many-problems-which-ones-can-i-make-a-difference-on.

Lewis, Michael. 2016. *The Undoing Project: A Friendship That Changed Our Minds.* New York: Norton.

Lord, Alexandra M. 2021. "Skill-Building and Thinking about Career Diversity for Graduate Students." In *The Reimagined PhD: Navigating 21st Century Humanities Education,* edited by Leanne M. Horinko, Jordan M. Reed, and James M. Van Wyck, 160–175. New Brunswick, NJ: Rutgers University Press.

Mainemelis, Charalampos. 2001. "When the Muse Takes It All: A Model For The Experience of Timelessness in Organizations." *Academy of Management Review* 26, no. 4: 548–565.

Martinez, A., and Brendan Byrne. 2023. "SpaceX Rocket Explodes Shortly after Test-Flight Takeoff in Texas." *Morning Edition*, NPR, April 20. https://www.npr.org/2023/04/20/1171023397/spacex-rocket-explodes-shortly-after-test-flight-takeoff-in-texas.

McAdams, Dan P. 2008. "Personal Narratives and the Life Story." *Handbook of Personality: Theory and Research* 3: 242–262.

———, Ann Diamond, Ed de St Aubin, and Elizabeth Mansfield. 1997. "Stories of Commitment: The Psychosocial Construction of Generative Lives." *Journal of Personality and Social Psychology* 72, no. 3: 678–694.

Miller, Alison B. 2008. *Finish Your Dissertation Once and for All! How to Overcome Psychological Barriers, Get Results, and Move on With Your Life*. Washington, DC: American Psychological Association.

Miller, Katharine. 2022. "Pioneering Tech Economist Susan Athey Joins Federal Antitrust Team." *Stanford Business*, July 7. https://www.gsb.stanford.edu/newsroom/school-news/pioneering-tech-economist-susan-athey-joins-federal-antitrust-team.

Mullaney, Thomas S., and Christopher Rea. 2022. *Where Research Begins: Choosing a Research Project That Matters to You (and the World)*. Chicago: University of Chicago Press.

Mullen, Ann L., Kimberly A. Goyette, and Joseph A. Soares. 2003. "Who Goes to Graduate School? Social and Academic Correlates of Educational Continuation after College." *Sociology of Education* 76, no. 2: 143–169.

Neck, Heidi M., Christopher P. Neck, and Emma L. Murray. 2018. *Entrepreneurship: The Practice and Mindset*. Thousand Oaks, CA: SAGE Publications.

Nori, Hanna, and Markku Vanttaja. 2022. "Too Stupid for PhD? Doctoral Impostor Syndrome Among Finnish PhD Students." *Higher Education* 86: 675–691.

Ph.D. Completion Project. 2007. "Ph.D. Completion and Attrition: Analysis of Baseline Program Data from the Ph.D. Completion Project." https://www.phdcompletion.org/quantitative-data/#.

Posselt, Julie R. 2018. *Inside Graduate Admissions: Merit, Diversity, and Faculty Gatekeeping*. Cambridge, MA: Harvard University Press.

Pulliam, Nicole, and Carolina E. Gonzalez. 2018. "Success or Fraud? Exploring the Impacts of the Impostor Phenomenon Among High Achieving Racial/Ethnic Minority and First-Generation College Students." *Journal of Access, Retention, and Inclusion in Higher Education* 1, no. 1. https://digitalcommons.wcupa.edu/jarihe/vol1/iss1/4/.

Reyes, Victoria. 2022. *Academic Outsider: Stories of Exclusion and Hope*. Stanford, CA: Stanford University Press.

Ries, Eric. 2011. *The Lean Startup: How Today's Entrepreneurs Use Continuous Innovation to Create Radically Successful Businesses*. New York: Crown Business.

Roberts, Emily. 2021a. "This Grad Student Eliminated Her Housing Expense to Pay Off Her Student Loans." Episode 8, September 27, in *Personal Finance for PhDs*, podcast audio. http://pfforphds.com/this-grad-student-eliminated-her -housing-expense-to-pay-off-her-student-loans.

———. 2021b. "This Graduate Student Launched a Passion Business Based on His Research." Episode 16, November 22, in *Personal Finance for PhDs*, podcast audio. http://pfforphds.com/this-graduate-student-launched-a-passion -business-based-on-his-research/.

———. 2022. "From Zero Funding to Graduating Student Loan Debt-Free." Episode 6, November 7, in *Personal Finance for PhDs*, podcast audio. http:// pfforphds.com/from-zero-funding-to-graduating-student-loan-debt-free.

Rohrbach, Augusta. 2021. "Out of the Field and Into the Woods: The PhD as Professional Compass." In *The Reimagined PhD: Navigating 21st Century Humanities Education*, edited by Leanne M. Horinko, Jordan M. Reed, and James M. Van Wyck, 55–74. New Brunswick, NJ: Rutgers University Press.

Sarasvathy, Saras. 2005. "What Makes Entrepreneurs Entrepreneurial?" Darden Case No. UVA-ENT-0065. Darden Business Publishing. https://store.darden .virginia.edu/what-makes-entrepreneurs-entrepreneurial.

———. 2008. *Effectuation: Elements of Entrepreneurial Expertise*. Cheltenham, UK : Edward Elgar Publishing.

Saxon, Jamie. 2022. "Inside 'The Looking Lab,' a Princeton Course Where Visual Arts Spark Entrepreneurial Thinking." Princeton University, June 21. https:// www.princeton.edu/news/2022/06/21/inside-looking-lab-princeton-course -where-visual-arts-spark-entrepreneurial.

Schultz, Robert, and Anna Stansbury. 2022. "Socioeconomic Diversity of Economics PhDs." Working paper. Washington, DC: Peterson Institute for International Economics. https://www.piie.com/sites/default/files/documents/wp22-4.pdf.

Schuman, Rebecca. 2013. "Thesis Hatement." *Slate*, April 5. https://www.slate.com /articles/life/culturebox/2013/04/there_are_no_academic_jobs_and _getting_a_ph_d_will_make_you_into_a_horrible.html.

Shakha. 2014. "Granovetter Rejection!" *Scatterplot* (blog). https://scatter .wordpress.com/2014/10/13/granovetter-rejection/.

Sidlauskas, Susan. 2017. "On Graduate Education: Is it Worth it? A Primer (with Memoir) for the Art History Graduate Student." *Rutgers Art Review: The Graduate Journal of Research in Art History*. Volume 32. https://arthist.net/archive/16085.

Sparkman-Key, Narketta M. 2021. "How to 'Boss Up' as a Black Woman in Academe." *Chronicle of Higher Education*, October 6. https://www.chronicle.com/article/how-to-boss-up-as-a-black-woman-in-academe?cid=gen_sign_in&sra=true.

Standlee, Alecea Ritter, ed. 2018. *On the Borders of the Academy: Challenges and Strategies for First-Generation Graduate Students and Faculty*. Syracuse, NY: The Graduate School Press, Syracuse University.

Stevens, Mitchell, Cynthia Miller-Idriss, and Seteney Shami. 2018. *Seeing the World: How US Universities Make Knowledge in a Global Era*. Princeton, NJ: Princeton University Press.

Swaminathan, Nikhil. 2012. "What Predicts Grad School Success?" *gradPSYCH*, September. https://www.apa.org/gradpsych/2012/09/cover-success.

Sword, Helen. 2023. *Writing with Pleasure*. Princeton, NJ: Princeton University Press,

Sylvia, Paul. 2018. *How to Write a Lot: A Practical Guide to Productive Academic*, 2nd ed. Washington, DC: American Psychological Association.

Taghavi, Aram. 2018. "Cory Booker's Mentor, Virginia Jones on Being Optimistic in the Hardest Times." *Medium*, December 4. https://medium.com/swlh/cory-bookers-mentor-virginia-jones-on-being-optimistic-in-the-hardest-times-9f3d4830755e.

Tello-Trillo, Sebastian, and Alex Hollingsworth. 2020. "Talking with Kelli Marquardt on Talking with People Outside of Your Field." Episode 16, September 16, in *The Hidden Curriculum*, podcast audio. https://podcasts.apple.com/us/podcast/s1e6-talking-with-kelli-marquardt-on-talking-with/id1526729667?i=1000491444632.

———. 2021. "Tips on How to Connect Research and Policy with Delegate Sally Hudson." Episode 16, February 9, in *The Hidden Curriculum*, podcast audio. https://podcasts.apple.com/us/podcast/e16-tips-on-how-to-connect-research-and-policy/id1526729667?i=1000508390139.

The Economist. 2010. "The Disposable Academic." December 16. https://www.economist.com/christmas-specials/2010/12/16/the-disposable-academic.

Townsend, Robert. 2021. "An Honest Assessment: The State of Graduate School Education." In *The Reimagined PhD: Navigating 21st Century Humanities Educa-*

tion, edited by Leanne M. Horinko, Jordan M. Reed, and James M. Van Wyck, 3–9. New Brunswick, NJ: Rutgers University Press.

Vaughn, Ashley R., Gita Taasoobshirazi, and Marcus L. Johnson. 2019. "Impostor Phenomenon and Motivation: Women in Higher Education." *Studies in Higher Education* 45, no. 4: 780–795.

Walkington, Lori. 2017. "How Far Have We Really Come? Black Women Faculty and Graduate Students' Experiences in Higher Education." *Humboldt Journal of Social Relations* 39: 51–65.

Wanzer-Serrano, Darrel. 2022. "All Aboard the Mentorship: A Discussion with Shantel Martinez and Bryant Taylor." Episode 2, August 31, in *Your Shadow Advisor,* podcast audio. https://www.yourshadowadvisor.com/episodes/all -aboard-the-mentorship-a-discussion-with-shantel-martinez-and-bryant -taylor.

Weisbach, Michael S. 2021. *The Economist's Craft: An Introduction to Research, Publishing, and Professional Development.* Princeton, NJ: Princeton University Press.

Wood, Maren. 2013. "The Afternoon I Decided to Quit Academia." *Chronicle of Higher Education,* August 8. https://www.chronicle.com/blogs/phd/the -afternoon-i-decided-to-leave-academe-and-what-happened-next.

———. 2019. "Dear 2004 Maren: Advice to My Past Self." Beyond the Professoriate, 2019. https://beyondprof.com/advice-to-my-past-self-l-maren-wood-phd/.

Yale Graduate School of Arts and Sciences. 2024. "Tuition, Funding, & Living Costs." https://gsas.yale.edu/admissions/phdmasters-application-process /tuition-funding-living-costs.

Yamada, Kobi. 2014. *What Do You Do with an Idea?* Seattle: Compendium.

Zounlome, Nelson O. O. 2020. *Letters to My Sisters & Brothers: Practical Advice to Successfully Navigate Academia as a Student of Color.* LTB Collective Books.

INDEX

academia: autonomy of, 11–12, 37–43, 55; contacts and networks in, 111–17, 133–34; corporate models of, 10–11; entrepreneurial mindset in, 13, 20, 39; hierarchical nature of, 41, 45–46; life outside, 50–51, 54, 58, 77–84; risk aversion in, 72–73; self-doubt and impostor syndrome in, 43–48, 55; traditional scholarship in, 10, 32–37, 50, 54–55, 94–95, 139–40; uncertainty in, 5, 12, 18, 23–24, 43, 60–66, 77–78, 83. *See also* entrepreneurial scholarship; graduate school; humanities, arts, and social sciences; ideas; knowledge production

academic capitalism, 10

admissions, to graduate school, 33

advisors: advisees' relationship with, 24, 39; negative impact of, 21, 23, 40, 101, 129; power of, 16, 24; role of, 16, 36, 38, 40, 42

AIDS, 82

Airbnb, 86

American Anthropological Association, 82

American Journal of Sociology, 76

American Sociological Association, 59

American Sociological Review (journal), 76, 120

Archives Month Philly, 136

Arriaga, Rosa, 76

arts. *See* humanities, arts, and social sciences

Association for the Sociology of Religion, 59

Athey, Susan, 64–65

The Atlantic (magazine), 71

Ato, Gladys, 77, 86, 88, 131–32, 140–41

autonomy: academic, 11–12, 37–43, 55; as feature of entrepreneurial mindset, 37–38, 50–51, 55

Ayn Rand Institute, 57

Bain, Ken, 93, 95–96, 99

Ballmer, Steve, 64

BCG. *See* Boston Consulting Group

Benor, Sarah, 92, 153–54

Berg, Maggie, 10

Bergman, Brian, 66–67

Bing, 65

SKILLS FOR SCHOLARS

www.ingramcontent.com/pod-product-compliance
Ingram Content Group UK Ltd.
Pitfield, Milton Keynes, MK11 3LW, UK
UKHW030914230225
455446UK00005B/19

9 780691 240886